IN THE SHADOW OF SARTRE

LILIANE SIEGEL

IN THE SHADOW
OF SARTRE

Translated from the French by
Barbara Wright

COLLINS
8 Grafton Street, London W1
1990

William Collins Sons & Co. Ltd
London · Glasgow · Sydney · Auckland
Toronto · Johannesburg

A CIP catalogue record for this book
is available from the British Library

First published in Great Britain by William Collins 1990
English translation © William Collins Sons & Co. Ltd 1990
Originally published in French as *La Clandestine* by
Editions Maren Sell © Editions Maren Sell 1988

Photoset in Linotron Fournier by
Rowland Phototypsetting Ltd, Bury St Edmunds, Suffolk.
Printed and bound in Great Britain by
William Collins Sons & Co. Ltd, Glasgow

To Dominique Hervé and François Truffaut,
exceptional interlocutors and friends
who are both dead.

A presence is so total,
Absence is so radical.

SIMONE DE BEAUVOIR

'For the appearance of an unexpected witness, an unknown photo, a recording of Sartre's voice have often come and upset whole sections of the enquiry. You think you understand, you think you know, and then suddenly an unforeseen document unsettles you, surprises you, and obliges you to start again from the beginning. Sometimes, on the other hand, it is a missing piece of the jigsaw that obsesses you, and haunts you until you discover it.'
ANNIE COHEN-SOLAL,
Sartre, 1905–1980

Here is one of the missing pieces of the jigsaw.

When I entered Sartre's life, apart from Simone de Beauvoir who shared it totally, there were four women in it. I was the fifth.

Each had 'her own Sartre', and even though from his point of view he remained fundamentally the same with them all, I know that his relations with each one were different.

My 'clandestine' situation gave me one advantage: I was to know everything; because we had to be careful not to give ourselves away, particularly when he decided 'to introduce me officially into his life', as he put it.

From that moment on, and until his death, I had a heavy burden to bear: ten years to hide.

In ten years there were many occasions when I might have betrayed myself. They created difficult situations that were sometimes comic, always unfair, and often painful.

I was never very happy whichever they were but I had no choice: one does not break with Sartre.

For a very long time I had considered it a tragic fatality that I hadn't been able to choose my sex. My mother didn't like girls or, more precisely, she couldn't bear the thought of being responsible for the future that awaited them.

'When you're poor you shouldn't have children, and especially not girls.'

Contraception didn't exist, and my mother was violently opposed to abortion. Her second child was a son, and it was with a heavy heart that she resigned herself to go through her five subsequent pregnancies, hoping that the babies would be boys.

'Men have much easier lives.'

This was her point of view; she had acquired it from her experience, and she knew what she was talking about.

I was her fifth child, and I am still convinced that her resentment increased as a function of the hope she built up each time of having another son. She had six daughters and one SON.

She called him my son, my king, my saint, until her death.

For many years I secretly dreamed of the sweetness of being chosen, and above all of not having to share. My fate was to be born the fifth; a curious coincidence gave me the fifth place in Sartre's life.

'You have a great advantage with me, you'll be
la petite dernière – the baby of the family. I've no
room for anyone else.'

For nearly ten years Sartre did his best to show me that he cared for me. I was always needing proof; it isn't easy to get rid of the ideas you have had from your early childhood.

Even though we met because of a letter I one day wrote to Sartre, I realized later that it was he, and he alone, who chose to establish a relationship between us and to make room for me in his life.

'Don't try to escape from your suffering; look for
its causes, and then destroy them.'

How could I have guessed what a long, painful effort would be needed before I discovered them?

I

1

When my brother told me that my mother was dead I felt like throttling him. Probably to make him eat the words he had just spoken, and stop him giving me the details that would force me to believe him.

But the word was out.

I shall never forget the colour of the sky on that 21 January 1960. A winter sky of the kind I used to like, china blue, such as you only see in the mountains. All the way to the rue Clauzel, where I was going to see my brother, his wife and their two children, I couldn't take my eyes off it. I had hesitated for a long time: should I go by métro? No, it was such a lovely day that I decided to go by bus, even though it meant changing twice. You just don't go underground when there's such a sky!

When I arrived my nephews made a big fuss of me. My brother was still in his pyjamas. My sister-in-law shared out the jobs to be done: she and I would go and do the shopping, and in the meantime my brother would lay the table.

I liked those streets in the 9th *arrondissement*. It was a lively district, I thought, and at that time there were still stalls in the streets where the women vaunted their wares in the working-class accent that was familiar to me. The two wicker baskets were soon filled. The light was so beautiful that I stopped at a flower stall and bought a

3

huge armful, being sorry that I couldn't get them to match the colour of the sky.

When we got back to the flat I found the room they used as a dining-room just as I had left it. My sister-in-law had gone into the kitchen to empty the shopping baskets. I was furious, and went to find my brother in the next room.

'That's really too much, you might at least have laid the table!'

He was sitting on his bed, by the telephone, looking haggard and greenish. He didn't say a word, but I knew at once what he was going to tell me. I felt my heart beating faster, I thought I was going to faint.

'Sammy, say something, don't just sit there ... Don't tell me Maman's dead!'

He stood up abruptly, covered his face with his hands and sobbed like a child. I threw myself at him, grabbed him by the throat and yelled, 'Tell me it isn't true, say it' – I was squeezing his throat as I shouted – 'say it isn't true ...'

He freed himself gently and took off his glasses. Not daring to look at me, after a long moment he murmured, 'A lady phoned: "Monsieur Sendyk? I'm calling you on behalf of your father. He asked me to tell you that your mother has died. He will call you later."'

I grabbed my coat and bag, and fled. I had a terrible feeling of helplessness. I knew for certain that my life was going to collapse, that I'd have to think everything out again.

In November 1959, I had taken my mother to the station. At the age of fifty-six she was travelling in a sleeping-car for the first time. Two months later, there she was in the cemetery in a sealed coffin.

Sleep deserted me. The only thing that helped me was

reading. I plunged into it desperately, and revelled in the morbid atmosphere of Samuel Beckett's *Malone Dies*. Its long questioning suited my state admirably. Naïvely, I thought I understood the novel. How stupid of me! At that time I didn't know how to 'read', I was too self-centred. Nevertheless, Beckett was my refuge. I lapped it all up. I read everything he had written, but every day I would go back to Malone with questionable obstinacy. But I had also just discovered Saint-Exupéry's *The Little Prince*, and paradoxically I found glimmerings of hope in it which began to help me out of my misery.

'What does "taming" mean?'
'It means creating bonds . . .'
'But if you tame me, we shall need each other. You will be unique in the world for me, and I shall be unique in the world for you.'
'If you tame me, it will bring sunshine into my life.'

From early morning, I began to be happy as I waited for the moment when 'the man I was in love with', my prince, would arrive. But was I unique in his eyes? No one is unique, except a mother . . .

I devoured Simone de Beauvoir's *La Force de l'âge (The Prime of Life)*, and came out of it amazed, overwhelmed, envious.

So someone really did exist who could say, 'If he told me one day to meet him exactly twenty-two months later on the Acropolis, at five o'clock in the afternoon, I could be sure of finding him there then, punctual to the minute. In a more general way I knew no harm could ever come to me from him – unless he were to die before I did.'

These words haunted me. Complacently, I saw them as the explanation of my despair: wasn't my unhappiness due to my mother, who had dared to die before me?

I realize today that this frantic reading was an escape: the moment I put the light out I saw my mother waiting for me at the window and waving to me interminably. I heard her say to anyone who happened to be there: 'Frankly, Madame, but quite frankly, have you ever seen anything more beautiful? Take a good look at her, from head to foot, it isn't because she's my daughter . . .' At the time I couldn't bear it when she gushed like this; she was tactless, I thought. But who would see me that way from now on? I felt she was present, although I knew that she was dead and I would never hear her again, never see her arriving or laughing or crying. Was it the fact of not having seen her dead that made it impossible for me to accept the idea of 'Nevermore'? It was all the suffering caused by this illusory presence, revived by the darkness, that I was trying to escape by desperately clinging to the light; that was what I was trying to forget by devouring book after book.

I started to read Paul Nizan's *Aden-Arabie*, which had a preface by Sartre. From the very beginning of this preface I had the strange feeling that these words were intended for me. I appropriated them, because they corresponded to my distress.

> 'We are stifling, from childhood people mutilate us . . . you are dying of modesty; dare to desire, be insatiable . . . don't blush at reaching for the moon. Don't try to escape from your suffering; look for its causes, and then destroy them . . . A young man came to see me . . .'

I finished reading it, put the book down, took pen and paper, and wrote to Sartre.

'A young man came to see me . . .'

I remember in particular two sentences in my letter –
which I posted at five in the morning, afraid I might
change my mind a bit later. The first referred to that
meeting on the Acropolis; the second, no doubt intended
to make a good impression, ended the letter: 'And don't
tell me that twenty is the best time in one's life.'

At that period I was desperate enough to be so crazy
as to write a letter to Sartre, to hope for an answer
without much faith, and yet to have the greatest doubts
that anyone could possibly be interested in me.

When my mother was alive, my son and I lived with
my parents in a little house in the 20th *arrondissement*.
I had no choice: when I separated from my husband I
couldn't afford to live on my own. But the four years I
spent with my mother were a time of real happiness.
Having dreamed of it throughout my childhood, at last I
had her all to myself.

Her sudden death had immediate consequences on the
organization of our family. It was decided that someone
must look after my father. As I was out at work all day
(I was a saleswoman in a luxury boutique and didn't get
home until the evening), my son went to school in the
neighbourhood and also needed someone to mind him.
In short, it seemed obvious to them that this should be
the role of my eldest sister, Fanny. So she and her husband
and daughter came to live in one of the two rooms in the
house. The other room was my father's. My son kept his
place. Knowing that she hadn't long to live, my mother
had often told my father, 'When I'm dead, I don't want
them to play football with my grandson.'

At that point I ventured to ask where they thought of
putting *me* . . .

The haste with which this decision was arrived at was no doubt due to the distress caused by my mother's death. The answer to my question was a vague 'We're sure to find a solution . . .' But there was no space for me in the house now. I was out on the street. I couldn't accept the idea of having to leave my mother's house. It seems squalid today, but the only way I could stay there was to sleep in the cellar. Which is what I did.

It was an old coal bunker. One part of it was below ground, the other was level with a kind of courtyard.

My sister Léa had painted the room. My father gave me an old bit of carpet, a wardrobe and a bed; my brother brought me a table and a chest of drawers.

The beaten-earth surface of the courtyard extended into a kind of rudimentary kitchen. Only a thin wooden door protected me from the elements. This kitchen of sorts opened on to the sole room, in which I lived. There was practically no daylight; I had to keep the only window permanently closed because it gave on to the courtyard. My fear of rats, of burglars, all the fears of early childhood resurfaced. As when I was very small, I even had to go out into the dark to go to the WC in the yard.

And yet, with the gradual improvements made by 'the man I was in love with', the place became almost habitable. I liked it when he was there, but found it unbearable when he wasn't.

I lived alone in this hole with my mother's dog, which I had kept with me: he spent the daytime on my bed, not even going upstairs, waiting for me until the evening.

When I came back from work I went into the house for a moment to kiss my son, who never came down to my cellar. Then I went 'home'.

But lately there had been a gleam of hope – although

impalpable, uncertain – in this misery: Sartre might answer my letter.

For weeks I lay in wait for the postman, whose steps I could hear in the street. Whenever he left anything, I rushed up and opened the letter-box. In vain. I received no answer from Sartre. I did my best to forget, and then one morning my father nonchalantly announced, 'Here, this came for you.'

'This' was a small white envelope. I turned it over to see the name of the sender and had some difficulty in hiding my emotion: 'J.-P. Sartre, 42 rue Bonaparte, Paris 6ᵉ.'

I looked for the date on the envelope, and discovered that Sartre had sent me this *pneumatique* giving me an appointment to see him forty-eight hours after he had read my letter.

My father had received it when I was out and stuffed it in his pocket, where it had remained all those weeks!

I held the envelope in my hand.

> 'Mademoiselle,
> J.-P. Sartre has received your letter and will be pleased to see you on Friday 22 July at 12.30, 42 rue Bonaparte (4th floor, left.) Please phone me to confirm the appointment.
> Claude Faux*

It was now September! I cried with vexation. I'd missed my appointment.

I made an effort to understand my father's attitude: why had he done this to me?

Our relations had always been very strained. He was

---

* Sartre's secretary at the time.

a cold, withdrawn man. My mother had worn the trousers in the family. She always wanted to have her own way in everything, and she did.

She had never allowed my father anything other than a subordinate role, and all her life she probably prevented him from expressing anything whatsover.

When my mother died I tried to draw closer to my father: I was implicitly asking him to replace her. It didn't work.

When I discovered that he had dared to deprive me of the long-awaited lifeline, Sartre's letter, I realized that this action was a kind of vengeance on the part of a frustrated man, a way of asserting his existence, even by such a negative act.

And Sartre: what had he thought?

He had thought, as he later told me, that I had either changed my mind or committed suicide. He had shown my letter to a graphologist friend and asked her opinion.

'Not only is this child in the shit but, if you want my opinion, she needs help quickly.'

I decided to write and tell him the truth. This time I lay in wait for the postman every day.

I grew impatient, felt sorry for myself, hated my father a bit more every day and then, full of resentment, did my best to forget all about it.

Quite simply, I didn't know that Sartre was not in Paris.

When the reply came I was too excited to read it at once. I delayed opening the letter. Finally I made up my mind to do so.

'Can you come on Thursday at 10.30 (in the morning).'

At eight o'clock I was in St-Germain-des-Prés.

I went and sat in a café and watched the passers-by. I would have liked to be capable of calling out to them and saying, 'Guess who I've got a date with!' They'd have thought I was a madwoman. What a pity! I would have liked to share my joy. I felt I loved them all. And yet the last time I'd been in this café I'd felt so alone and terrorized. The news was coming over the radio, the café was packed and everyone was silent. They were waiting for the landing (in the Algiers *putsch*). But today all that seemed very far away; St-Germain-des-Prés represented my meeting with Sartre.

The time passed too quickly, but when 10.30 came I nearly abandoned the whole thing. But in the end I slowly climbed up the four flights, waited outside the door for an eternity, and then made up my mind to ring.

I heard footsteps on the other side of the door and thought my heart was going to stop beating. I would have liked to vanish into thin air . . . Too late. Sartre was standing in front of me.

I began to feel less distressed when I thought, as I looked at him, 'The photographers try their best to make him look ugly but he isn't ugly. The ones who don't like him probably misrepresent him deliberately.'

'I'm glad you came.' He invited me in with a gesture. 'Come into my study, we won't be disturbed there. Sit down.' He pointed to an armchair. 'I'm afraid I haven't anything I could offer you to drink at this hour.'

He walked round his desk, and sat down too. His deep voice made me feel even more intimidated. I didn't speak. He looked at me, and waited in silence. After a long moment I heard him say, 'Well, for someone who wanted to see me, you haven't much to say for yourself. That is what you wanted, isn't it?'

I was paralysed, incapable of uttering a sound.

'Come over here. I'll show you something.'

He went over to the window and opened it.

'Come over here. There's a fine view.'

I too stood up, and joined him.

'Look, that long road is lovely. That's the Gare Montparnasse* at the end. It doesn't always look like this, but today, with this light, this blue sky . . .'

'I hate the sky when it's blue.'

'Really? And why is that?'

'Because at the end of every winter my mother used to go to the window when there was a blue sky and say: "I've got through another winter".'

'You know, I was beginning to think I would never hear your voice. Would you like a cigarette?'

He was back in his chair, and offering me a dark blue packet that I was seeing for the first time.

'They're big, your cigarettes.'

'Yes, it's real tobacco. I'm sorry, they're all I have.'

Three short rings on the bell made me jump in the middle of a sentence. Sartre stood up.

'We'll continue our conversation some other time. That's a promise, and next time I will get in touch with *you*.'

He went over to the door and opened it.

'I'm not early, I hope?'

'No, no, you're exactly on time, Castor, as usual.'

'If he told me one day to meet him exactly twenty-two months later . . .'

A lump came into my throat.

'Liliane Zziegel,' said Sartre.

---

* This was the old Gare Montparnasse, which was not in the same place as the one that was built later.

'How do you do, Mademoiselle,' said Simone de Beauvoir.

I went down the four flights slowly, assigning a sentence to each step. How beautiful she is, said my left foot; how simple and nice he is, said my right foot. When I got outside, the light dazzled me. I crossed the rue Jacob and looked up at the church clock: it was one thirty-five. I was in the clouds. My thoughts were chaotic. Images of the past were confused with those of the present. I saw myself as a little girl, hiding when I came out of school. The 'dirty little yid' who was overcome with shame at the idea that a real image could be put to the insults hurled at her – her father and mother shouting out in the street 'Old clothes for sale!' – was today proud, and dying to shout out to everyone that she had seen Sartre and Simone de Beauvoir, that they had spoken to her and that she was going to see them again. So she wasn't as contemptible as she had so often been told over so many years.

I went home and made a scrupulous note of my first three hours with Sartre.

'We'll continue this conversation, that's a promise,' Sartre had said. I clung to these words, and refused to give credence to the idea that he might break his promise. But after two weeks of waiting, I began to have doubts.

At that time – and things haven't changed much since – I attached absolute value to his every word. I never stopped telling myself: he promised. And so when I heard his voice on the phone I was both astounded and resentful enough not to be able to utter a sound.

'I haven't forgotten you, I would like to see you but I haven't much time. Tell me how you are. I'll arrange things so that I can find a moment. Look after yourself, I'll see you soon.'

I have often thought back to that phone call. At the time I was certain that I'd wrecked everything, but now I'm convinced that Sartre would never have sent me a *pneumatique* so soon after if he hadn't understood what my silence concealed.

I held his letter very gingerly. The writing was beautiful, and very easy to read. This surprised me. I discovered his concern for precision, and it amused me: twice, after 10.30 and 11.30 – 12.00, he wrote 'in the morning'. I didn't then know that he used to make appointments with his close friends for very late in the evening.

> 'Can you come on Thursday at 10.30 (in the morning), I know it's inconvenient for you.* But I want to see you very soon, and that's the only time I can manage. If it's all right – and even if it isn't – don't bother to answer: I shall be here working in any case, so you won't be 'standing me up', but just phone around 11.30 – 12.00 (in the morning) to make another appointment. I look forward to seeing you again and I'm glad you're working.'†

When I rang at his door for the second time I had the pleasant feeling of being expected. Sartre opened the door almost immediately. He shook my hand firmly.

'I like people to be punctual. Come in, you know the way. Sit down.' He sat down too. 'You weren't quite yourself the other day, were you?'

'I was surprised. To tell you the truth, I wasn't expecting to hear from you again.'

---

* He said this because he imagined that I was like various women in his life who had nothing to do and got up late. Not knowing me, he wasn't aware that I had a job and got up early.
† For Sartre, 'to work' meant 'to write'.

'You mean, you *were* expecting to. You mustn't take it amiss, my life is very full.'

'But . . .'

'Don't say "but", it's stupid. I was worried to feel you were so upset on the phone, so as you see I've fitted you into my work schedule.'

'You shouldn't . . .'

'Stop talking nonsense. When you start something you must go through with it. Tell me something about yourself. As you see, the sky is blue again, you'll have to learn to get used to it.'

'I suppose that will come . . .'

A sudden noise made me jump.

'Take no notice, my mother has probably taken it into her head to do a bit of housework. Well, that's something new – you can actually smile. What are you smiling at?'

'I don't know, you . . .'

'ME?'

'Yes, everything is so simple with you. You . . . your words . . . I didn't imagine you like that.'

'And how did you imagine me, then? As a stiff-necked gentleman who uses abstruse words, sits on the edge of his chair and is self-satisfied or pompous?'

'Not quite that, all the same.'

Sartre looked at me with a smile.

'Don't worry, I'm pulling your leg. I know what you mean. But the thing is, it's the people who come to see me who are intimidated – it's not that I try to make them feel uncomfortable. And anyway, it's tiresome, it's a great waste of time.'

'It isn't so simple . . .'

'What isn't so simple?'

'You aren't just anyone . . .'

'If I was "just anyone", as you say, you wouldn't be here. What do you say to that?'

'*Oh là là* . . .'

'What is it?'

'I think it isn't so simple . . .'

'But of course it is, it's quite simple, I only wanted to know how far I could go. But don't worry, that's just my way. After all, I hardly know anything about you.'

Sartre explained that he was going away for two weeks, that he would like to see me when he came back if I wanted to, and made an appointment to meet me in the Pont-Royal bar at four thirty in the afternoon. That day he explained his timetable to me in great detail.

'As you can see, there really isn't any room for you. Come on, don't look like that. If you can manage it we'll see each other on Tuesdays from half past four to eight o'clock. That's the only time I have.'

2

Sartre's life was organized with absolute precision.

There was, of course, the immutable time he spent with Castor, and he spent most of his time with her.

His working hours were sacred, it took a totally exceptional event to make him cut them by even a few minutes. Then, as he said, there was Wanda's time, Michelle's and Arlette's and Evelyne's time. And finally, mine.

We met on Tuesdays at half past four, as I have said, at first in the Pont-Royal bar or in cafés.

Sartre didn't want me to go to the rue Bonaparte in the afternoons because he wasn't alone and he was afraid we might be disturbed.

Later he was forced to leave the rue Bonaparte – his flat was bombed by the Algerian colonists' secret army, the OAS – and I went to fetch him wherever he was living.

From time to time he invited me to lunch with him, explaining that Michelle or Arlette was not well, or more often away. At that time he was living on the Right Bank with Castor, and we lunched in that district.

When he moved into the Boulevard Raspail things

became more complicated, for me at any rate, as will become apparent.

Sartre had described his life to me in detail, told me that he lied to everyone except Castor, that he would tell me everything, but that no one other than Castor* was to know that I existed.

Seeing my amazement, Sartre explained that he wanted peace more than anything else, that it had become a habit, and that anyway all these lies rather amused him and added a touch of spice to certain relationships that had become a little stale.

When I asked him why he preferred to hide me he looked at me with a mischievous smile and said, 'You'll see, soon you'll want more, and as I've fitted you into my work time because I have no other, if one day, having told you that you will be *la petite dernière*, I tell you that there's another, you'll start making scenes and, as I've said, I want peace.'

Sartre was particularly good at getting people to talk. He detected the slightest pretence, the smallest lie, he interpreted silences, observed facial expressions, went through everything with a fine-tooth comb. He made no concessions, harked back to a phase, demanded fuller information. 'I don't understand you, there's a detail missing. If that was what was said to you, what precisely had you said before?'

He wanted to know all or nothing.

One letter from the late sixties gives a particularly graphic example of this need to question, of the insatiable curiosity that was characteristic of him:

> I don't understand a thing – as always with your
> first account of something. I'd have to ask you

* And all Castor's friends, who included Evelyne.

IN THE SHADOW OF SARTRE

some questions. For instance: is something upset-
ting you (I mean, apart from this business)? Where
do you eat? Why do you say, 'I don't feel blame-
less', when your letter is a double justification: of
yourself, and of his* behaviour? What was he
doing in the 'dive'? Were there girls there?
Or some of his mates? Why was he so desperate
since he had, after all, contrived to stay there?
And didn't he perhaps invent (just a little) his
terrible boredom to justify the fact that he was
spending his nights in a bar? What kept him there
until five in the morning (eight hours on end)?
What did he spend there? Why did the front
tyres (*both at the same time*) burst? (Too old, or
what?)

... Unless I know all that, I can give you
neither an opinion nor any advice: do realize that
I'm sorry about this, my poor child. But I can't
possibly know whether he deliberately ruined his
holiday (against a background of boredom and in
a difficult situation, that I grant) and had you find
him like that, or if there really was no other way
of killing time. In actual fact there were *a hundred
other ways* but not for him, and in any case that's
what worries me.

... if you have told me *everything*, I can't see
why you feel you're at fault ...

... you did everything you could to send him
to the sea, in a place he once liked.

... You joined him there – and left him your
auto, which was a way of not leaving him quite
alone ... He asked you (he was right) to pay

---

* He was referring to my son, Gérald.

more so that he could have his own room, and you agreed; you found a bill for extras (cleaning, meals at odd hours) and will pay it without protest (in actual fact, did you protest?). I don't think anyone could do more.

And this time you haven't told me anything about yourself (which you must admit is pretty rare). It's all about him. I'd have liked to know how things were *for you*. How you got on in Bandol . . .

I can only imagine that things weren't too bad, since you stayed there . . .

Write to me when you get this letter. I'm worried about you (I was slightly irritated at first, because you didn't give me enough information to go on so that I could understand what had happened, but then my affection got the upper hand, child, and I am *with you*.) I imagine that you're now with 'your man' (as you call him) and that it's doing you good.

With much love

He answered all my questions in the same way. Before Sartre moved into the Boulevard Raspail, as we met in cafés he mostly questioned me about my family, my background, my job, 'the man I was in love with' (as he put it), my son Gérald, who was then nine years old, and especially about my mother's death. My shyness gradually disappeared, I found it easier to talk, and I began to enjoy our meetings and conversations. When Sartre told me he was going on holiday I felt despondent.

'Poor child, you came into my life too late.'

I felt that things had got too much for me. Everything

was happening so quickly. I had never imagined that Sartre would assume such an important place in my life, and in such a short time.

I felt all sorts of different things. I was flattered that he took an interest in me but I didn't understand in what way I could interest him.

I was afraid that when he thought it over during his long absence he would decide that I was too uneducated and superficial, and change his mind.

At that time I had no idea of how much and in what way he could become interested in people.

I knew he told Simone de Beauvoir in detail everything he did without her. I had admired her enormously for a very long time, and one day I plucked up courage and asked Sartre what Simone de Beauvoir thought of our relationship.

'She's delighted to know that you work and earn your own living, and that makes her very well disposed towards you.'

At the time I thought this answer somewhat limited. Sartre, who had a habit of observing the slightest reaction on people's faces, quickly added, 'You'll realize later that that's an excellent beginning.'

We'd meet before he went on holiday, he would do his very best.

'I'll write to you. You can write to me and phone me in Rome after 20 August.'

I hadn't dared ask Sartre why he was imposing this restriction on me: it was only the end of June. I was disappointed, I felt I was being thrown over, and could do nothing to change the course of events. This feeling of being powerless upset me. I made a great resolution: I wouldn't write.

In spite of the relief I felt in moving into a pretty little flat* after his departure, I was miserable. In a letter dated September 1962, Sartre wrote:

' ... from your last letter you don't seem to be terribly pleased with the flat you wanted so much. Is it because in spite of everything you feel more alone there than you did in your cellar? Are you still writing? You know, there were quite a lot of things I liked about your first attempt. You don't mention it any more and I'm afraid you might have lost heart. We'll talk about it again in October: you must go on with it. My very best wishes.'

I was very impatient in those days, I liked dramas and decisions, my holiday had been planned and I left for St-Tropez with a heavy heart.

In spite of all my efforts to try to ignore the letter-box, I couldn't manage to.

I went through feelings of doubt, certainty, hope, neglect, desertion, betrayal. I watched for the postman enthusiastically, gave up sadly, pretended to be resigned. I didn't then realize that my resentment made Sartre seem even more present.

Convinced that I was doing the right thing, I wrote to

---

* A former pupil to whom I had taught yoga in Cuba got my address from the Véga bookshop in the Boulevard Saint-Germain. (This bookshop used to specialize in esoteric books, but it no longer exists.) He invited me to lunch and told me he was leaving for the United States to join his wife, who was expecting their first baby. He hoped to resume his yoga classes when he returned to Paris in a few months' time. I had to tell him that I was living in a cubbyhole and that in order to earn my living I had become a saleswoman. 'What a pity, Liliane,' he said, when we parted.

A few days later I received a letter enclosing a cheque for 10,000 francs: 'I'm sorry, my dear Liliane, not to be able to do more, but I hope this will enable you to find somewhere to live. I'm looking forward to resuming your invaluable yoga classes. With best wishes ...'

The great generosity of this man – who is still my friend – radically changed my life, and never failed whenever I was in trouble.

The first letter from Sartre to Liliane

The first dedication from Sartre to Liliane (1961)

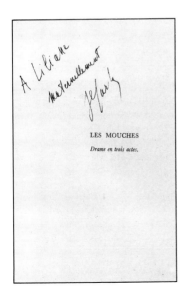

Photograph of Liliane
taken by Sartre in 1963

LES MOTS

A Liliane, la petite dernière,
pour fêter le deuxième anniversaire
de sa naissance, j'offre cette frère
histoire de sa famille paternelle (en
particulier de Lizas celle de ton arrière grand
père Schweitzer que tu n'as pas connu)
Ton frère qui t'aime

Sartre in his new flat in the Boulevard Raspail. On the polished wood table lie his packet of Boyards, his ever-ready chequebook, a science-fiction novel by Jean Ray and a volume of Flaubert. Then there is Castor's table, the standard lamp bought at the flea market, and the bed, behind the sliding door which was never closed.

Sartre, cut my holiday short and returned to Paris. A letter from Sartre was waiting for me there:

'Friday 29 [August 1962]

'I've been meaning to write to you for a long time to explain things and apologize: I really thought we would be able to meet before I left and then I didn't have time. Naturally I haven't written: I always have to make an effort to write letters, I don't know why. As soon as I'm back (around the 25th [September]), I'll drop you a line and we'll arrange to meet, if you want to. You say you are demanding. But that's not it. You have too much time and I haven't enough, that's all. With best wishes.'

A few days later he phoned me from Rome. He'd received my letter, he was very sorry that I had come back in such a bad state, he had certainly not forgotten that he had promised to write to me. He hadn't done so but he would explain later.

On his return from holiday that year Sartre had moved into a studio flat in the Boulevard Raspail, and I went to see him there. I was surprised at the contrast. In the rue Bonaparte the room he worked in had a splendid desk, imposing bookshelves, and the whole atmosphere was what I thought appropriate to a writer.

The room in the Boulevard Raspail in which Sartre received me was very light. In front of the french window there was a tiny desk, quite unremarkable, cluttered with books and papers, cigarettes and ashtrays, pens and a lamp; it looked like a toy to me. On the right there was a larger, white-formica table against the wall, with a window above it. There was a chair, also white, in front of it; I deduced that this was where Sartre wrote.

There were little shelves here and there along the big left-hand wall, which looked as if they were about to collapse under the weight of the books. There were vast quantities of books on the floor. A nondescript-looking armchair stood in a corner.

Behind a sliding door, which I never saw closed, there was a bed.

Sartre picked up the white chair, put it in front of the little desk and asked me to sit down. He grabbed a wooden chair, shiny with age, which was conspicuously out of keeping with the undistinguished quality of the rest of the furniture, and sat down in his turn.

Sartre noticed the way my gaze lingered on the chair.

'Do you like it? It belonged to my great-grandfather. This chair is the only thing I care about – except my books, of course.'

'It's very beautiful, but it looks uncomfortable.'

'I like it to be uncomfortable, I don't like seats that corrupt.'

I was quite overcome at seeing Sartre again; intimidated, at a loss, scared. I felt he was deliberately waiting for me to speak first. He was amused by my embarrassment, there was a mischievous look in his eye. I was very close to tears; I think he took pity on me.

'What's the matter?'

'I don't know. All this is so unlike you . . .'

He pretended not to understand, and came to my aid.

'Oh, you know, so long as I can work in peace, and then there's the view. I like being on the tenth floor, and I like cemeteries, too.'

I hated cemeteries. This one, the Cimetière Montparnasse, extended as far as the eye could see, it was full of trees of all species, still green, either lined up along the pathways or concealing the graves, and there were flowers of all colours. It didn't seem right to me; it didn't look as if it was made to 'shelter' the dead.

'It doesn't look like a cemetery from here.'

'You'll see; it looks totally different in every season. Quite soon it will be brown and gold, then the trees will lose their leaves and there'll be practically nothing to see but the graves; the paths will become sinister, rectangular roads. When it snows, it's even more striking. In spring it's superb, it changes almost every day. I know it very well; Castor lives opposite, as you know, and you can see it from her bathroom window. We have the same view, but from a different angle. But you don't give a damn, you're not with me. You're a curious little person. I thought you'd be pleased to see me but no, you're sulking. What's wrong?'

With infinite patience and skill Sartre gave me confidence and got me talking. He steered the conversation with ingenuity and bombarded me with questions. Sartre knew what I had come for. After our second meeting he had offered me my first dedication:

'To Liliane, maternally.'

Shortly afterwards, Sartre suggested that I should also come on Thursday mornings between nine thirty and eleven. It was only later that I understood the reason for this marvellous gift.

Sartre had arranged to meet me in a café.

'We'll have breakfast together.'

'You know very well that I haven't eaten breakfast since my mother died. She used to bring it to me in bed.'

When the waiter came up to us he ordered without consulting me, which was most unlike him.

'Two double espressos and four slices of bread and butter.'

I swallowed a few mouthfuls with difficulty.

Sartre gradually got to like these breakfasts, which later became more frequent, and I know for certain, because we often spoke about it, that he decided to have breakfast in order to teach me to start eating again.

This was my first – unintentional – intrusion into his life.

In the cafés and restaurants where we met during the first two years, dialogue predominated. We were getting to know one another; that was what I naïvely imagined. In actual fact Sartre already understood everything, he knew what I was made of. And that was the question: what could he do to help me to recover? How easy and gay everything seemed to me at that time, when I was with him!

After Sartre had moved into the Boulevard Raspail, where I used to visit him, the dialogue disappeared. He would ask precise questions, and confront me with truths for which I was ill-prepared.

'You're confusing things. The cause of your present distress is your mother's death, but distress and grief have nothing to do with "suffering". At the moment it's blinding you, and that's only natural, but you must try and discover the real causes, which lie in your early childhood. You must understand that they are directly linked with your refusal to accept your mother's death, to accept death, that is. We shall also have to understand why you are so mistrustful and 'abandonic'. You may not be conscious of it, but the word betrayal crops up too often in our conversations.

'I know; when you were very small, when you were in hiding during the war, you lived with the fear of death, and this reality, for it was one, was abominable. We'll come back to that later. But before the war, when you were very very small . . .'

'I don't remember anything before the war. Oh yes, I do: something my mother said once when she was propping herself up against a wall, just before she collapsed and fainted.'

'What did she say?'

' "I knew it! He's got me pregnant again." '

'Are you sure of that? And what makes you say it was before the war?'

'I remember it in Yiddish, that's not something you invent, and my last sister was born in 1937. There were no more children born after her. I can see the place, it was when we were living in a shack in the slums. Before the war we were in the shack, after the war it was a stone house.'

'Say it in Yiddish.'

'*Her ott mo choïn vido que marcht a kint.*'

'And what did you think at that moment, the moment your mother lost consciousness?'

'How should I know! I must have been very frightened, I've always been frightened, I'm always frightened of everything.'

'How can you tell me that you've always been frightened when you've just said that you don't remember anything about when you were very small?'

'I tell you, I've always . . .'

'It's very irritating of you to be so obstinate. Don't you realize that this is the only way to see things clearly, that this is the way we shall make progress?'

I wasn't prepared for this sort of relationship. I always came off badly in my timid attempts at rebellion. I was well aware that I irritated Sartre with what he called 'my false certainties, my faking and my assertions that weren't based on any precise facts'. My last resort was tears.

'Come on, you know I'm on your side. I know all this

is difficult, but when you put your mind to it you're quite capable of understanding the facts. For instance, you said just now that your relations with your mother were a mixture of generosity and demands that you sensed as blackmail because she knew she hadn't long to live, and that at the same time you were terrorized by her fits of temper. Did you always remain passive in those situations? What did you feel?'

'When I was small, until I was twelve or thirteen, I often felt I hated her. You'll think it stupid, but I wanted her to love me, and above all to prove it to me. I couldn't see her violence as being anything other than hate, I know now that it wasn't, but that was what it felt like at the time. The idea of blackmail came later, when we'd been told that the slightest vexation could kill her. Yes, I was passive, I used to sulk, I felt misunderstood and unhappy. What do you think I could have done? The slightest attempt at rebellion earned me a beating. I preferred being beaten to being shouted at, but unfortunately the two always went together.'

'She had a terrifying life . . .'

'Yes, I know that now, but I can't help it, I can't bear being shouted at. When you're a bit short with me, when you get angry, I feel threatened, I say to myself, "Any minute now he's going to throw me out!" I have the impression that my heart's going to stop beating, that I'm going to die, in some way.'

Sartre smiled, a kind, affectionate smile.

'You're going to enlarge on my sadism! Don't be afraid, you foolish little thing, I've already told you that when one undertakes something one must see it through to the end. It's true that you sometimes irritate me, but I still like being with you.'

3

Our conversations were resumed every Tuesday. I was once again teaching yoga, so my time was my own.

Without fail, Sartre would study my face and then say either, 'Things don't seem to be going so well today, you've got your stubborn look on,' or, 'It looks as if things are going quite well today.' And while giving me the illusion that the conversation arose quite naturally, I know he used to steer it wherever he wanted.

When Sartre observed that it was twenty past eight (we left his flat at precisely half past eight because I used to walk with him to Castor's, where he spent the evening and the night), he would invariably put his hand on my arm and at the same time say, 'There now, you're a good girl and I like being with you.'

At the beginning I was so busy being sorry for myself and feeling misunderstood, and above all I was so totally exhausted after those four hours with Sartre, that he might just as well have said, 'You're a bloody half-wit and I never want to see you again,' and I wouldn't have noticed the difference. Two or three years later, I don't remember which year it was, when Sartre looked at the time I put my hand on his arm and said, 'There now, you're a good boy and I love being with you.'

We laughed a lot that evening, and for the first time we seemed to get to Castor's much too quickly.

On Thursday mornings I used to meet Sartre in the café at half past nine and we had breakfast together. I felt I had grown wings, I was in good spirits, and Sartre observed that the bread and butter disappeared.

'I'm not so generous as your mother, I should be quite incapable of making coffee for you, and even less capable of bringing it to you in bed, I'm too clumsy.'

'But you've chosen both generosity and terror with me, as she did.'

'For the moment, yes. Later, we'll see. But you must admit that what you most lack is a father.'

After breakfast I walked back with Sartre to his flat and we parted in the street, not bothering about who might see us. Wanda, Michelle and Arlette all got up late.

'If you're feeling so cheerful because of being seen with me, you must know that I don't like that.'

'To a certain extent it is, yes, but it's mostly the fact of not having to hide. Yesterday, you know, when I passed you with Michelle and I was forced to ignore you, I got into a panic, it was as if my life depended on it. I had my nightmare again. This time I was in the métro, there were a lot of people, I was wearing the yellow star, and all of a sudden a man began yelling, "For yids, it's the last carriage!"'

'I know, I was sorry about that, but I've already told you that as soon as I can I'll introduce you officially into my life. You see what you're like: we were enjoying being together and you choose the very moment we're going to part to tell me the most important thing.'

'I didn't choose it, it just cropped up. If I'd said it when I arrived you'd have said severely, "Stop complaining, I know all that."'

'Nothing ever just crops up, you'll realize that one day.

Come up with me, I can't let you go with such ideas in your head.'

Sartre was annoyed; he had spoken in a very curt tone of voice. I followed him. In the lift going up to the tenth floor, naturally I imagined that I was in for a bad time. Sartre was silent, and I began to panic. Shutting the door to his flat, Sartre asked me to sit down at Castor's table, gave me his newspapers – we bought them together on our way to the café – and said affectionately, 'Sit down there, do what you like but above all don't interrupt me. We'll be able to talk a little later. For the moment, I have to work.'

I moved the chair a little so as to be able to see Sartre without disturbing him. He sat down at his desk, lit a cigarette, got out his pen and immediately began to write. From time to time he gave a vague little cough; I didn't even dare to swallow. I watched Sartre. He was unpredictable; I had expected the worst and he was offering me the best. To watch him write was a privilege I had often dreamed of. As everyone close to him knew, Sartre was inflexible where his work was concerned. No one ever disturbed him unless something happened which, in his opinion, couldn't wait. And of course, he was the one who decided. From time to time he crumpled up a sheet of paper covered with his beautiful handwriting, threw it into the waste-paper basket and started writing again. I hadn't stopped watching him, yet I jumped when he put his pen down and turned to look at me.

'Well, child, as you see, I don't wish you any harm.'

From that day on, Sartre invited me to stay with him until one o'clock every Thursday morning. I gradually allowed myself to be tamed, I read the papers, I was at my ease. Sartre always stopped writing early enough to give us time to talk a little.

'Well, child, what are you thinking about, then?'

At that time I was incapable of expressing any feelings whatsoever. I would have liked to tell Sartre how happy I was with the favour he was doing me, and how I appreciated it as the most wonderful present he could possible give me. Instead of which, I answered, 'I can't understand why you insist on writing at that lousy desk, there isn't even room for you to rest your arms on it.'

Sartre's face hardened. He looked at his watch.

I added, 'That's not all I'm thinking about, but I'm thinking that too.'

'That's better. Go and buy me one, then, I'll give you some *sous*. I'd like it to be big, unostentatious, made of wood, but above all not new!'

'A beautiful big old table with a thick top and four nice straight legs, is that right?'

'That's right, but you'll have a job to find one like that!'

'If I'm not mistaken, I've had a narrow escape! It's a good thing I opened my mouth before you did!'

'There's something in what you say!'

We parted in fits of laughter.

The following Tuesday I was delighted to be able to tell Sartre that I had found the table at the flea market, and I described it to him. He was delighted.

No one, apart from Castor – that went without saying – was to know how he had acquired this table. That was his first thought. Even though all his close friends knew that Sartre was not the man to go and buy anything for himself, apart from tobacco, books, newspapers, records and writing-paper. He would have to invent a lie, but that rather amused him. He even went so far, as I later discovered, as to invent several lies, one for each woman, and that amused him even more. He never gave himself away.

Sartre explained that it was out of the question for the table to be delivered during the time set aside for Wanda, or Michelle, or Arlette. That would cause trouble, and he didn't want to be disturbed during his working time.

'I'll ask my brother, next Tuesday, in *my* time, half past five, will that suit you? Don't worry, he'll come on his own. We've already discussed it, he's just waiting for your agreement.'

I'm still amazed at my brother's generous discretion. He transported 'the colossus' by himself to the door of number 222 Boulevard Raspail and up the two steps into the building, carried it across the hallway to the lift, got it into the lift, and then managed to get it out again. When he rang the bell, Sartre opened the door to a man dripping with sweat but smiling at him despite being out of breath. The table was standing on its short side, which made it taller than the door; it was blocking the landing.

'Come in, have a rest, have you really brought that monster all by yourself? I'm so sorry, I didn't imagine, I don't know how to thank you . . .'

'You already have, by what you've been doing for my little sister all this time.'

We had cleared the space where Sartre wanted to put the table. My brother had polished it. Sunlight was flooding into the room, making the wood the colour of honey. I shall never forget Sartre's pleasure as he looked at it in front of the french window. He stroked the wood, bent down to examine the legs, felt the thickness of the top, and then began all over again.

'It's exactly what I wanted, you're a couple of angels and I shall never know how to thank you. Go and fetch a couple of beers, child. Do you like beer?'

I darted into the kitchen and came back with the beers.

'Do you know that you called me *tu*?'

'You deserve it – just look at that lovely table!'

I felt a completely new kind of happiness. I couldn't say when it awoke in me, but I felt it every time the situation lent itself to such a feeling. You make yourself at home with people as best you can.

When my brother had gone, Sartre took the lovely wooden chair, sat down at the table and laid his hands flat on it.

'What a wonderful present you've given me, child. Whenever it gets too cluttered we'll tidy it together; it belongs to us both.'

'Do you know the story about the man who decides to change the wallpaper in his bedroom?'

'No. What's the connection?'

'When the wallpaper's been changed, he discovers that the carpet's disgusting, so he changes it. Pleased as anything, he goes into his room, looks down and sees his old slippers on the beautiful carpet . . .'

Sartre laughed heartily.

'What do you suggest? I'm listening.'

'Wooden bookshelves from end to end of the long wall, and from top to bottom. I'll get the carpenter to come and measure up during my time, and they can be put up when you're away on holiday.'

'But that'll mean a lot of work for you!'

'Let me do things for you, please. As for the reciprocating you're always talking about, we've got a long way to go yet!'

Sartre told me of Castor's enthusiasm. She thought the table superb, and had asked him to compliment me on it.

I have never met anyone who so appreciated the slightest little service as Castor and Sartre. Nothing escaped their notice. 'Thank you a thousand times, you're an angel, it's going to give you a lot of work, won't it be too tiring?' If they had only known what joy it gave me!

Some time later Sartre said to me, 'I have a mission for you, my poor child. Castor hasn't been able to stand the white formica table since I've had my desk. Could you find her one in polished wood?'

Within a few months Sartre's flat was unrecognizable. The carpenter had covered the big walls with bookshelves in a wood that matched that of the table, and my son had helped me arrange the books. I found a rustic floor-lamp in the flea market, then a very small, very tall table in the same wood as Sartre's desk, and finally a chest. I bought big grey stoneware ashtrays.

I never knew how Sartre explained his new interior to 'his ladies', and I still wonder how Arlette, who was so suspicious, swallowed the tale Sartre told her. All the changes were the work of a woman; for anyone who knew Sartre, that was obvious.

4

Of the women 'established' in Sartre's life about whom he spoke to me in detail, neither Wanda nor Michelle bothered me. Evelyne was the only one I knew, and Sartre had told her everything about me. I liked her beauty, her lively mind, her intelligence, her warm presence, her way of reassuring you with a squeeze of the hand or with a look. It took me a very long time to get over the shock of her death.

Arlette, on the other hand, whose fits of anger Sartre feared, gave rise to many different feelings in me. I identified myself with her. She had met Sartre only a short time before I had, and in the same way, after writing him a letter, and she was Jewish. Wanda and Michelle had known him much longer, and were older. In spite of himself, Sartre fomented my jealousy when he tried to persuade me of his affection by saying, 'If only you'd written to me earlier! I can't change anything now.'

As I have already said, I found sharing very difficult. I equated the strength of Sartre's feelings with the amount of time he gave to each of us, and I didn't think his allocation was fair. And yet he was not sparing of expressions of his affection for me, as can be seen in this letter, written in the summer of 1969:

... Why do you sign yourself *'ta toute petite'*? If it's an affectionate expression, that's fine. But if it's to tell me – and I'm afraid it is – that you have only a very small place in my affections and my thoughts, how wrong you are, my little girl. After I got the first letter you wrote me here, which was so gay, I have been thinking affectionately of you all the time, and I have even told you so: that's the way I love you – very much. And I have imagined the face you had all that time, that softened, relaxed face, with a hint of something secret in it and a private little smile, that I feel like kissing on its sweet cheeks. At the moment you're suffering a slight regression, as you do every year about this time.

Why, *toute petite bête*, do you have to crucify yourself over trivial matters? I felt the fit coming over you at the *second* phone call. You were pleased with the first: you imagined, *I don't know why*, that I wouldn't come back until October. With the second you'd forgotten that, and you said to yourself: he could have come back for *my* Tuesday or *my* Thursday: he would have done for one of the others but *I* get treated like a bit of shit, etc.

Which is not true, because if I had come back earlier it wouldn't have been only you but the *others* who would have seen me earlier, and my return on Thursday doesn't suit anyone. So you are *just like everyone else*, and the reason I'm not coming back earlier is because there are things I want to finish, an interview with *Il Manifesto*, appointments I put off until the last week so as to get as much as possible out of Rome. Having said that, believe it or not, it so happens in this month of September 69 that you are the one I most want to see, (perhaps) because I haven't seen you for so long but especially because your holiday and your very frank letters have given me the impression that now you'll be able to show some joy instead of fidgeting on your chair, twitching or poker-faced and boot buttons where your eyes ought to be. It's true: I'm not particularly looking forward to coming back and at the moment the idea of seeing you is the pleasant little light, the only little warmth that enlivens my dreary return.

As for my health: good. What am I doing? Working and reading detective stories. *Petite idiote*, you *know* that I'm very well, and as for telling you about my life in Rome, whether happy or monotonous, you know too that it's nicer to do so in person.

... Goodbye, *ma toute petite* – I say it with affection.

With love. I'll phone you on Thursday and come and see you on Friday.

I'm reading the Trotskys, that's what you ought to wade through (3 volumes, 650 pages each, but it's the whole history of the USSR) as soon as I'm back, it'll take you six months.

I don't remember in what circumstances I first met Arlette.

I had waited so expectantly to meet her that it all took place in a kind of haze; I didn't listen to anything Sartre and she were saying, I didn't see her. One detail struck me though, and finished me off: her hair was tied back. So she obeyed him. How many times had Sartre not told

Liliane photographed by François Truffaut

The first street sale of *La Cause du Peuple*, on the avenue du Général-Leclerc. Sartre is in the foreground, followed by Castor, Truffaut and Jean Moreau.

Sartre's seventieth-birthday party at Liliane's, 1975. Castor never stops making us laugh.

Liliane and Castor at the Récamier Theatre, 21 June 1977. The photograph was taken by Gérald, Liliane's son.

me, 'I don't understand why you insist on having a fringe which makes you look stubborn and stupid, whereas I think you're rather intelligent.'

From that day on, every time I met him I put slides in my hair so as to leave my forehead uncovered. This detail was not lost on him, and delighted him.

To bring our meeting to a close Sartre stood up and said rather sheepishly, 'I'm afraid it's time for us to part company . . .'

I found the reality of this unbearable: I was the one who had to leave. I stammered, 'Yes, I'm sorry . . .'

All this time I had been forcing myself not to call him *tu*. When he stood up I was horribly tense. I shook Arlette's hand, but when Sartre held his out to me I vowed to myself, 'I'll never do this again, never.'

On my way home I began to worry. 'Arlette knows Sartre as well as I do; it's not possible that she didn't sense his embarrassment. If she is as suspicious and as much of a "cop" as he says, she'll have understood everything.'

And she probably did understand everything that day, but she couldn't afford to break with Sartre.

I went on my way, perturbed. 'He calls her "child", he probably also tells her that she is *la petite dernière*, just as he tells me. What am I to him, then? Isn't all this a lie? Can I still have confidence in him?' All my old fears were returning . . .

I got home, my son was waiting for me, eager to hear the result of this interview that he had so dreaded for me. We had talked about it a lot. Instinctively he found the right words.

'Listen, I'm an only son, and all my life I've dreamed of having to share things. Try not to think about it. It's so wonderful to have Sartre for a friend. That's what counts!'

But for me, that first meeting remains the day when I discovered that just like me, he called Arlette 'child'. Sartre seemed amused by the importance I attached to this discovery, the cause of my making a furious scene, to which he put an abrupt end.

'At least that way I'm not likely to get it wrong!'

'One day you'll call me "child" in front of her. A lot of good that'll do you!'

'You know, you won't get a chance to see her with me so often. She doesn't like sharing.'

'That's one thing we have in common.'

'And also being Jewish.'

'Yes, but look, out of five women, you have three who're Jewish. That can't be an accident . . .'

'Jewish women have a look in their eyes that I particularly like. You can read their whole history in those eyes.'

II

5

Tuesday was the day Sartre lunched with Arlette. We saw each other immediately afterwards. He had put me on my guard and asked me not to show myself. I couldn't help always arriving outside his building early, though. Arlette walked back with Sartre to his door. I suffered lamentably from the 'time' she was robbing me of. I would hide behind a big tree the moment I caught sight of them, thus plunging myself even deeper into clandestinity.

This 'persistent determination to make myself suffer', as he called it, both saddened and irritated Sartre. 'But it's no great hardship to ask you to arrive at four forty!'

He finally persuaded me. But one Tuesday when I was late because I'd been held up by a passing demonstration, I ran into the lobby and came face to face with Arlette and Sartre, who were waiting for the lift. It was raining that day.

Terrified, I walked up to the first floor and went into the pathology laboratory, came out immediately explaining that I'd come to the wrong floor, and sat down on a step one flight up. I don't know how long I stayed there sobbing. I didn't know what to do. Had they gone up to the flat? I was trapped. I went home, firmly determined to break with Sartre.

Sartre phoned me. He was dismayed and worried. He

had gone downstairs, looked for me in the cafés and feared the worst.

'Don't move. I'm coming to your place.'

He arrived at six o'clock, he hadn't found a taxi, there had been traffic jams because of the rain and the demonstration. I had found the waiting unbearable. It had transformed my 'determination' into anxiety, and allowed my habitual passivity to regain the upper hand.

'Poor child, it's all very unfair but it won't happen again, I promise you.'

'My father promised, too, but that didn't stop him having me taken into care.'

'Into care? But you never told me that. And when was it?'

'When I was three and a half.'

'Three and a half?'

'Yes, when my sister Odette was born, she's three and a half years younger than me.'

Big tears were streaming down my face, but I couldn't produce any kind of sound.

'Don't cry, not like that, I'm genuinely fed up, believe me, I promise you . . .'

'People always promise, everyone promises, no one understands what a promise means. When you make a promise you ought to keep it.'

'But why were you taken into care?'

'Because we were poor, and there were a lot of us, and my oldest sister, the one who brought me up, was only twelve or thirteen, and my father couldn't look after us . . .'

'Did they come and fetch you, then?'

'No, it was even worse than that. My father took us to the Hérold Hospital, all five of us. I remember it perfectly. We were sitting on very low, polished-wood benches.

44

In front of us there was a woman behind a kind of booking-office window with a little oval door – well not quite, but an unusual shape – a door the woman opened when she was talking to someone. At one point she said, 'Monsieur Sindyk' – all the anti-Semites always called us Sindic instead of Sendyk. My father stood up, I was holding on to the bottom of his jacket, I walked over to the window with him. They talked, it seemed to me for a long time. I couldn't follow it. I was too little and I couldn't see the lady any more. We went and sat down again, and another lady came. She was wearing a funny little white hat and she had a kind of dark-blue cross on her chest. It was only when she turned round that I saw it was a big cape. She wanted to take me by the hand. 'Come with me, dear,' she said, but I clung on to my father's legs. Then she said, 'Fanny, Samuel, Bella and Léa, come with me, say goodbye to your papa.' They stood up and I saw them disappear, all four of them.'

'And then?'

'And then?' I was crying, and couldn't go on. 'Then my father went out into the hospital courtyard, I was still holding on to his jacket. There was a big van there with a huge red cross on the back. A man opened the door and it intrigued me that the cross was cut in two. It's a very persistent memory, that cross cut in two. Inside this van there were benches on either side. When I saw them I began to scream. I clutched my father's legs … he unclasped my hands and the lady took me in her arms. I squirmed and screamed.'

I was blinded by tears, the emotion was too much for me. I stopped speaking. Sartre took my hand.

'Go on, it's very important.'

' "Don't leave me, Papa, don't leave me!" I talked very well, I could talk very early.'

45

'And then?'

'Then my father promised me – he promised, you understand – that he'd come and take me home. I shouted: "When?" and he said: "Soon, I promise." "When's soon?" I asked. "Tomorrow?" And he said: "Yes, tomorrow."'

'How long did you stay there?'

'A long time. My mother had a pulmonary complication, she was in hospital. I seem to remember, I'm not certain, having been taken to visit her in our hovel by a lady who took me home with her afterwards. Yes, I remember now, I was very well dressed in white, that was the first time.'

'You must go and see your father and ask him whether all this is true. I have the feeling it is, but it's worth checking. But actually, you had another sister? Did you go back into care?'

'Probably, I don't remember.'

'That's odd; you were older! It'll come back to you. What were your feelings at that moment, and who were they directed against, your father or your mother? Try to answer me.'

'It's difficult to say. I had a feeling of being rejected, I imagine, but that was permanent, or maybe it came from that event, if I can call it that. Today, frankly, I think it was directed against my mother, I don't know why, it doesn't seem logical, but it's what I feel. Though maybe it's the fact that I've never been able to forgive my mother for having abandoned all six of us during the war – Pauline was already dead – when she was trying to get my father released.'

'Abandoned? Where, and to whom?'

'To nobody. She sat us all down in a semi-circle on the floor in the shack, she was crying terribly. When she'd managed to stop crying she said, "Your father has been arrested by the Germans. Life without him doesn't mean anything to me. You must stay here, I'm going to Évreux to try to get him out. If I don't, they'll kill him. I'd rather die with him. You, Fanny, you're the oldest, you must look after your brother and sisters. Don't move from here. If I'm not back in two days it'll be because they've arrested me, and in that case you must take the children to my sister's.'"

'This is frightful, what you're telling me, why haven't you ever mentioned it during all the time we've been talking to each other?'

'I've told you so many things. Actually, it has only this moment come back to me. I suppose I'd buried it. It was very present while my mother was alive. Since she died it only comes back in my nightmares. It was too difficult to live with. I was torn between two equally strong feelings. I wished she would die – that would punish her – and I was terrified at the idea that she might.'

'She did come back, of course?'

'No. She sent us word that she'd managed to get my father released, an old man was giving them shelter, and she asked Fanny to take us, the three little ones, to her sister, and then go and join her with Sammy and Bella.'

'I have to go, child. You must go and see your father. Phone me at Castor's as soon as you've seen him. Be well, I shall get you out of all that, we're on the right road.'

I went to see my father and told him the Hérold Hospital story in detail.

'What a memory you have, it's incredible, you were so little.' He seemed to be very proud of me! 'You're asking me if it's true? But of course it's true! You hung on to me so, you yelled so, I couldn't get rid of you!'

When I left my father I walked for hours, sobbing,

haunted by his words: 'But of course it's true!' When I got Sartre on the phone I was completely drained; drained, and in revolt.

'Well then, you see, child, if it hadn't been for that encounter, which seemed to both of us to be disastrous for you, I mean the one yesterday with Arlette, we wouldn't have got where we are. It's hard for you, I know, but it's going to help us more than you think. I'll explain tomorrow morning. Be well, I'm fond of you, you know that, and I'm pleased with you.'

The following morning Sartre, as usual, scrutinized my face. His look was benevolent.

'Well then, child, how did you spend the evening and night? Badly, I imagine? But tell me, there's one thing I don't understand, why were you separated from your brother and sisters when you were in care?'

'They went with the big ones; I was too small. I'm sure it would have been different for me if I'd stayed with them. As you know, I was very fond of my sister Léa. If only they'd let her stay with me!'

'I understand now why you are "abandonic" and mistrustful. The importance you attach to promises struck me right from our second meeting.'

'Abandonic?'

'Yes, abandonic. How many times have you begged me to let you leave first? Don't you remember? In the street, in a café or a restaurant, it irritated me, I thought it was a crazy idea: to go in together and then wait until you'd left before I could go. So Castor was right when she said, "Look for signs of abandonment. I mean, in her early childhood. It seems to me that this young woman, who has accepted responsibility for her own life – she works, she's bringing up her child on her own – is abandonic. That would partly explain why it's so difficult

48

for her to grieve for her mother." After all, is there a worse form of abandonment than that of a mother's abandonment of her own child?'

'It's true that I can't bring myself to forgive her.'

'To forgive her for what?'

'For being dead.'

'She didn't choose that, after all!'

'Yes, she did. She used to cry and say, "One day I shall eat my fill, and then I'll die, Professor Le Nègre said so, but at least I shall have eaten my fill once in my life." '

'You never told me that!'

'Before the war we were very poor. We ran up bills with all the tradesmen. My mother used to send my sister Léa and me out to try and get bread and milk on credit. It worked for a time; it's harder for people to refuse that sort of thing to two little girls, but it wasn't long before we were getting sworn at: "Tell your dirty yid of a mother to go and get some bread from her own country!" After that there was the war, we were in hiding and didn't have any ration cards. My mother denied herself for us, and my father too, I suppose. There were five children to feed.'

'Five? How come? Seven, you mean!'

'No. My little sister, the last one, died in 1940, and my sister Bella had been deported.'

'But she was deported in 1943 – that's what you told me.'

'Yes, but there wasn't enough room where my parents and the older ones were hidden. Léa, Odette and I were in Paris with my mother's sister, I told you that on Tuesday. We were apart for over a year.'

'You mean to say you stayed in Paris with your aunt for a year?'

'Yes. My mother, my father, and the three older ones,

including Bella, were in Évreux, that's where she was recognized in the street by a woman who denounced her to the police and they arrested her.'

'What was she doing in the street? You told me they were in hiding.'

'They were. But she'd persuaded my mother to let her go and sleep with a friend so that we could come. There were five girls to one folding-bed; it was feasible with four, and my mother finally said yes. It became an obsession. For fifteen years my mother never stopped saying, "If I'd said no, she'd still be alive.".'

'Let's come back to your mother. Why do you say she chose to die?'

'When Bella was deported, my mother was very ill. At that time you couldn't go out any more, not even to fetch the doctor. All Jews were arrested, women, children, whether French or not. After the Liberation my father, but especially my brother, began to earn some *sous*, and you can just imagine how we fell upon the food, and my mother had a coronary. She was admitted to hospital and when she came home she wasn't allowed salt, bread, meat, butter, cheese – she wasn't allowed anything! She would weep in front of her bit of skinned chicken and refuse to eat boiled vegetables. "I'm being given grass to eat," she would say. And she said a hundred times, "One day I shall eat my fill, and then I'll die, but at least I shall have eaten my fill once in my life." '

'And that's what she did?'

'Yes. Léa and I went to see the lady at the hotel where she was staying when she died at Amélie-les-Bains. She told us that my mother sent my father out to play cards every evening. The moment he'd gone, she would go down to the kitchen and give Madame Vial a demonstration of Jewish cooking. That was what she missed,

Jewish cooking, and naturally she did herself proud. One evening my father came back and found her all alone – dead. When they left – I mean, my father alive and my mother in her coffin – Madame Vial found a whole heap of forbidden delicacies under her mattress. She'd said she would do it, and she did.'

'And she even allowed herself the luxury of leaving you with a image of her alive! Have you visited her grave?'

'No, never, and I never shall!'

'You will, you must, I'll come with you, it's necessary . . .'

Sartre looked at his watch.

'Time's up, child. We'll come back to the subject.'

'Don't go – *please*.'

'We'll leave together. I must go. You can come with me as far as the door. Don't be afraid, I've no intention of dying.'

Sartre went into the lobby of his block. I saw him from behind on the other side of the glass door, he turned, raised his arm, waved to me for a long time and then disappeared.

I stood there, paralysed, facing the door, and shivered in spite of the mild May weather. The last time I had seen an arm raised like that had been in November 1959, on a station platform, and it was my mother's arm.

6

I was longing for the next Tuesday, but I was also dreading it. I was afraid of the mood Sartre would be in. In actual fact he was always the same, observing the expression on my face, the intonation of my first words, or my stubborn silence. During the whole time that I presented myself to him in this state – and it lasted for several years – I came up against terrible fits of anger. I tried to explain to Sartre that it was precisely his way of scrutinizing my face, his harsh answers or his silences, that paralysed me.

'You'll never understand. It's precisely the opposite. It's you, and you alone, who oblige me to be disagreeable. I feel I'm wasting my time! You make too much of it. You turn up and look as if you're saying, "See how unhappy I am!" It's unbearable. Get this straight, child: you can tell me, "I'm feeling bad," and we'll discuss it. But once and for all, either stop indulging in that sort of attitude or don't come any more.'

I was shattered, obsessed by certain words that I transformed so as to give them an irreversible meaning. I interpreted the rapidity of my heartbeats as the certainty of instant death, and I was overjoyed. That would teach him – he'd see whether it was an act!

'Oh, come on, child, say something, do something. It's your passivity again – I'd like to know its origin, so I could help you get over it. What are you thinking about? You're outraged, you hate me at this moment, but you don't say anything. Aren't you capable of getting really angry for once, then? Do you realize that you're turning this anger in against yourself, and that it's hurting you? Come on, child, make an effort, you know I don't wish you any harm.'

Sartre had been deliberately brutal. He knew, as had often been the case, that I would need time to understand what he was trying to tell me and to be able to discuss it calmly.

'Just look what a state this desk is in. Come on, we'll put the books away.'

'You know what you are – you're a dictator!'

'And your mother, what was she?'

'A Cossack!'

'Why are you laughing?'

'I thought you were going to say, *"Et ta sœur?"* [meaning: "Get lost!"] Don't ever tell me again that I'm a good girl. After all you've just thrown at me, I shan't believe you. I really wonder what you see in me!'

'I see you as a good person.'

'Oh yes? More like a poor sucker.'

'No, I mean it: fundamentally good, and for me that's a very fine quality.'

'You're having me on!'

'No, I'm very serious, believe me.'

Sartre was standing on his chair. He handed me down some books and asked me for others.

'You're too quick, I can't keep up.'

'I thought I was supposed to be passive?'

'Don't talk rot . . .'

'I was joking.'

'It's true that you're quick, but not always quick enough

for my liking. It'll take you at least a week to admit that I'm right . . .'

'Don't start again, that's enough for today.'

'Yes, you're right, that's enough.'

Sartre got down from his chair.

'Look, that's very good, don't you think? We'll finish it some other time.'

There were three short rings on the bell. Sartre went and opened the door.

'Welcome, little Castor!'

She had come to fetch Sartre. They were dining in a restaurant that evening.

Castor noticed that the desk had been cleared of all its clutter, and said gaily, 'What a good idea of yours that was, I congratulate you!'

'We'll do that once a month, won't we, child?'

'At your service, Maître!'

Castor smiled politely.

Sartre laughed heartily and said to her, 'I'll explain.'

I went home crushed under a feeling of great lassitude and the certainty that I would never get Sartre to understand that he was wrong.

As soon as I left him I felt anger rising in me.

'Aren't you capable of getting really angry for once, then?'

Every word came painfully back to mind; I could hear the curt way he had spoken to me. 'He doesn't have any respect for me. He doesn't understand, he doesn't want to understand. But why do I put up with it all?'

I got home. My son was on holiday. I was alone. My dog made a fuss of me, I picked him up, he buried his head in my neck.

'At least you make a fuss of me, you're always pleased to see me.'

I caught sight of my face in the mirror.

'Don't take on that victimized expression. Don't take on these eloquent looks. It's unbearable, it's monstrous. Talk! Come on, child, you know I like being with you.'

As if the last words wiped out all the others ... and I had this evening to live through. What do people do to stop thinking of something and get themselves to think of something else? Was I a freak? Sartre found fault with me for everything.

'What did you have for lunch, child?'

'A small steak and a salad ...'

'You're making yourself out to be a victim again. You'll never learn!'

Seeing my amazement, he added, 'You ought to have said, "Steak and salad," and to have let me ask you, "A proper one or a small one?" Don't you understand the difference?'

That was how it had all begun. He had got irritated with me and I had got obstinate. When people raise their voices I retreat into myself, as he knows. We have often spoken about it. If he had explained it to me differently ...

'Don't fake yourself, child.'

Even when he's absent, he's present. I'll never make it!

7

One day Sartre informed me that he was going to Russia, but that he would only be there five or six days. I protested.

'OK, but after that you're going to be away for months . . .'

'Oh, come on, child, do I reproach you for living a love story?'

'Ah, it's a woman you're going to see? Is it serious?'

'Yes, but keep it to yourself. I have enough problems with my lot as it is. Incidentally, would you be the woman to find me some black astrakhan skins, enough to make a coat, but it's absolutely essential for them to have a Russian stamp on them. I'll give you some *sous*, it doesn't matter how much they cost, they're for Wanda, I've bartered the skins for peace.'

'Of course. I just hope peace exists, but how are you going to get round the others?'

'Badly. By the way, child, I mean to adopt Arlette, but I'll never do so without your consent.'

I felt myself growing pale. My heart beat faster.

'You're joking. Are you serious? Why would you do such a thing to me? Adopt anyone you like, but not Arlette! You never stop telling me that it was unforgivable of my mother to prefer my brother to me, that it will take you years to free me from my need for proof that irritates you so much, and now you suddenly announce, in the middle of a story about astrakhan skins, "I'll be away next week," and in the same breath, "I mean to adopt Arlette . . .", as if you were asking me to get you some shaving-soap . . .'

'You know very well that it doesn't mean anything to me.'

'How could I know that? And if so, why do it?'

'It's complicated. I'll explain.'

'You'll explain, you'll explain, that's how you always get out of things! Do you realize what you've just told me . . .'

'I tell you, I'll never do it without your consent . . .'

I was trembling all over, my head was swimming, big tears rolled down my cheeks.

'Don't cry, child, not like that, but tell me . . .'

'Stop telling me, "Don't cry like that." It's the only way I know how to cry, and anyway I don't cry so very often . . .'

'That's true. And anyway, it won't happen right away, and I've told you, I won't do it without your consent.'

I'd stopped listening. I didn't want to hear any more.

'Calm down, talk to me, for goodness' sake, say something!'

I thought of the conversation we'd had the previous day, and I couldn't bear it.

'You'll see, when I've officially introduced you into my life and you've got to know Arlette, you'll discover that your place in my life is just as important as hers. Quite simply, though, you arrived later and I had hardly any room left. Don't forget that I fitted you into my work time and kept you there. That ought to prove that I really care about you.'

The day before! We had had that conversation the day

before . . . Since when had he made this decision? No, it wasn't possible, he didn't lie to me . . . He couldn't have had this idea in mind, and . . . Or else it was to prepare me . . . I'm going mad, yes, that's what's happening to me, it's all muddled up in my head, if I can't trust him any more, I can't trust anyone . . .'

'You know very well that I'll never give my consent. You're crafty, you're a fine one to tell me what to do. And Castor, what does she say about all this?'

'She disapproves. She says I'm going to damage you and Evelyne.'

'Oh yes, that's true, there's Evelyne, poor Evelyne! Have you told her?'

'No, not yet. I tell you, I'm thinking of doing it, but it won't happen right away.'

I was hunched up in my chair, rocking back and forth, furiously tugging at my lower lip. I was no longer with Sartre, I was in a big dormitory, I think it was in a town hall. It had a very high ceiling, there were a whole lot of white cots on the marble floor. We were all in care, my sister Bella (the one who was exterminated in A.), Léa, Odette and I. My father had volunteered for the army on the declaration of war. He wanted to defend France. To his mind, that was the least he could do; it was his country, he had been made welcome there and allowed to stay. True, there were anti-Semites who insulted him and told him to go and feed himself in his own country, but he didn't make generalizations. Not all Frenchmen thought like that, and France was his country. My mother was in despair: 'You'll get killed, the Jews will be the first to be sent to the front. If you die I shall kill myself, I can't live without you.' My father was obstinate, and gave priority to his sense of duty and of gratitude to France. My mother uttered the worst threats, shed floods of tears, but in vain. I don't remember all the ins and outs of this new ordeal. My resentment probably locked it all up inside my head. Once again my brother had preferential treatment – he stayed with my mother. It was out of the question for her to be separated from him. My oldest sister, Fanny, also stayed at home, she was indispensable. I felt compassion for her, she was everybody's servant.

This time the abandonment was double: my father 'chose' to get himself killed for France, and my mother got rid of four of her children. I decided to refuse to eat, I'd end up falling ill, she'd come and fetch me, or perhaps I'd manage to die. In the evenings, when the lights were put out, I fought against sleep. I knew that a supervisor came round holding a torch which she shone full in our faces, the old cow, to make sure that all her charges were asleep.

After so many years, I suddenly found myself plunged back into that dormitory where one night I had desperately waited for the supervisor to come. She hadn't wanted to understand my mute appeal any more than Sartre had today. When she discovered that my eyes were wide open she flew into an indescribable rage. She jerked back my blankets and screeched, 'Ah, so you want to defy me, do you? You won't go to sleep. I'll teach you to have some respect, you dirty little yid!' She took the trouble to pull back my night-dress and gave me the most monumental smack on the bottom that I have ever received, in front of the frightened eyes of the whole dormitory, which she had woken by her yells.

I didn't shed a single tear, I wasn't going to give her that pleasure. And I wouldn't go to sleep either . . .

You always do fall asleep in the end. In the early morning I thought I had dreamed that my father had whistled (he had a very special way of whistling to let us know that he was home), I leapt out of bed – it was already light – and ran barefoot to the big staircase. I remained rooted to the spot; Bella and Léa had joined me and were standing beside me. A soldier was running up the white stairs. I threw myself into his arms, buried my head in his neck and knocked his cap off. My two sisters were tugging at him, the little one had followed us and was shouting, 'Me too, me too!' My father put me down on the stairs and took Odette in his arms. How handsome I thought him, my papa! He had got permission to come and say goodbye to us before leaving for the front.

Sartre put his hands on my shoulders.

'Come on, child, tell me what you're thinking about.'

I just about managed to look up, and answered, 'I'm not thinking, I'm feeling very small, that's all.'

'We're always thinking about something.'

I clammed up again, and wept in silence.

'Do you realize that you're doing violence to me?'

After a very long silence, I said in a muffled voice, 'But why? Why?'

'Because I'd told Arlette that I'd called it quits, but I shall certainly have to tell her about Lena* sooner or later. All this is just 'social', you know that, child. It doesn't take anything away from you, and you know how I loathe the social.'

'Well, what a nerve! You loathe the social. All this is just social, you say, but you do it just the same! You were the one who wrote, "Only acts count," and what is there to justify such an act, seeing that you loathe the social?'

I'd said this so calmly that I was amazed at myself.

'You wouldn't be able to understand. When I tell you

---

* The woman he was going to see in the USSR.

that what matters most is to be left in peace, basically it's
the truth. But it's more complicated. You'd have to know
all about Arlette and all about me to be able to understand.
And anyway, I'm not sure I understand it myself. I have
to deal with the most urgent things first, of that I am
sure. But time's up, child, don't be obstinate, we'll talk
about it some other time, try not to be too miserable. I've
told you, I won't do it without your consent.'

'You know very well that I'll never give it to you!'

'Are you going to give me a lift, or are you too angry
with me to do me that favour?'

'I'll do you that favour, even if it won't give me any
pleasure. All the same, you might have waited till you
came back to tell me that! Though perhaps you did it
deliberately, for my own good?'

'No, certainly not.'

Sartre put his hand on my forearm. I stiffened.

'Believe me, I'm really sorry. It's true, I ought to have
waited until I got back. I would like you to understand
that it won't take anything away from you, quite the
opposite, you'll be my bastard, and I much prefer bastards
to adopted children.'

'Ask Arlette to understand. After all, you've a perfect
right to screw anyone you want to!'

'It's not a matter of screwing. I shall see Lena as often
as possible . . . That will cause trouble . . .'

'You got yourself into it!'

'Ah, so it was I who went looking for you all?'

'At any rate, you made a good job of seeing that we
didn't leave you!'

'That's better; you're getting some of your spirit back
. . . Come on, child, let's make it up, you know I don't
like it when we part like that. Forget all about it, and
anyway we're going to see each other on Thursday.

Promise me to be well, I'm fond of you, you know I am. After all, it's better to have a bastard father than no father at all!'

'I have got a father . . .'

'If he can be called that . . .'

'By the way, hasn't Arlette got a father either?'

'Of course she has!'

'Then why don't you find her a mother? It's enough for me that you replace my mother, it never crossed my mind that it should be made official!'

We had reached Castor's block. I got out of the car and opened the door for Sartre – this had become a habit – when I saw Castor leaning out of a window, watching us.

I was worried when she suddenly asked me, 'Is everything all right, Liliane?'

'Yes, Castor, everything's all right. Why? Are we late?'

'It's a quarter to nine, I was getting anxious.'

I said goodbye to Sartre and left in a pitiable state. My son wasn't there that evening, and I was relieved to be alone. I took a sleeping-pill and fell asleep at once.

8

Every so often Sartre would choose what he thought was an opportune moment and patiently return to the delicate question of the adoption. 'Well, child, that consent, have you been thinking about it?'

I would invariably retort, 'Yes, yes, but the answer hasn't changed, you know, and it isn't likely to.'

Sartre never went beyond that.

Today, thinking back on it, I reproach myself bitterly for having tormented him for so long by my obstinacy. I can see his face again, with a fleeting expression of distress giving place almost immediately to one of reflection, as if to say, 'Let's leave it at that, I shall find a way,' and then he would finally cut things short and tell me, 'You aren't the type to give in. Right, let's say no more, there's no great hurry.'

More and more frequently Sartre told me that he was going to the USSR. I knew he met Lena there and I was delighted for them, although my 'abandonism' inevitably got the upper hand again. At that time I was incapable of forgetting myself (as he put it), and showed my resentment awkwardly: I kept quiet.

Invariably, Sartre became violently irritated.

'You're monstrous. You claim to be fond of me but you always prefer yourself. You're all the same: everything for yourself and nothing for the other person. I've told you how fond I am of Lena. Have you so little generosity towards me that I have to put up with that pathetic face every time? After all, you have your own life, and I approve of it! Imagine for a moment that you were separated from X by a three-hour flight, which you wouldn't even take anyway; you know all the difficulties that such a journey which has to be official entails! I have to juggle with time, take my whole brood into account, can't you understand that, child? I've already told you, I shall see Lena as often as possible. All it takes away from you is a Tuesday and a Thursday, and don't forget that I don't know if I shall be able to go back there, or when!'

'You're right, it is monstrous. I am pleased for you, you must believe me, but that always comes second. My first thought is always, "That's it, he's leaving me again." It disgusts me to be like that but I don't think I can help it. I'm not proud of myself, you know! I wonder if it'll change one day?'

'We'll get there. It takes time, that's all. And anyway, I know very well why you're like that. I got angry, but I don't really think you're monstrous. Cheer up, you're not a bad sort!'

Every time he went away, Sartre sent me a telegram to let me know he'd arrived safely. Postcards and short letters allowed me to know where he was. I thought about him with tender gratitude. And indeed, I finally understood that you can be separated for a time from someone you are very attached to and yet not be too depressed, provided the other is happy.

In 1964, Sartre and Castor managed to get permission to bring Lena to Paris for three weeks. So Sartre informed 'his women' and me that he wouldn't be seeing any of us during all that time.

While Lena was there, Sartre phoned me two or three

times a week. Everything was going well for him, and for me that was the essential. I thought I was beginning to feel what Sartre had taken so long to try to make me understand: you have to learn not to prefer yourself.

On the first Tuesday I spent with Sartre after Lena had gone, I questioned him eagerly. As usual, he replied readily. He hoped to go back to the USSR at Easter, but he didn't know how he was going to square it with Arlette. She had taken Lena's existence and being ousted herself, albeit temporarily, very badly.

'Then you haven't taught her not to prefer herself?'

'She thinks that I preferred myself!'

'If I understand rightly, things went rather badly?'

'To say the least.'

'You look fed up.'

'It always makes you fed up when you hurt someone you're fond of.'

'It'll sort itself out . . .'

'It'll sort itself out, as you say, and then there'll be other hassles.'

'What exactly are you trying to prepare me for?'

There were three little rings at the door. Sartre stood up.

'Have you been saved by the boxer's bell?'

Sartre laughed heartily, and opened the door to Castor.

9

A few months later a kind girlfriend phoned and advised me to go and buy *France-Soir*.

'Sartre has adopted a daughter, did you know? It's on the front page.'

I didn't finish my yoga class that evening. I felt the earth was opening up under me, I couldn't breathe. I collapsed on my bed, sobbing. He had promised! Without my consent . . . I must have repeated those two phrases for hours on end. Then I phoned Castor. She was alarmed; I couldn't get a single word out.

'Liliane, what is it? Talk to me, get a grip on yourself.'

'He said . . . he said, Castor, that he'd never do it without my consent!'

'Ah, so you know. He wanted to tell you himself . . .'

'But he promised, Castor . . .'

'Come on, calm down, you know very well that it doesn't mean a thing to him.'

'He'd promised, Castor.'

'He'll explain it to you. Do please calm down, all this is 'social', it doesn't count, you know how he loathes it and how fond he is of you . . .'

'But he said he would never do it without my consent . . .'

'Are you alone?'

'Yes.'

'It's late, Liliane, take a sleeping-pill, you can talk about it with him tomorrow. Are you listening to me, Liliane?'

'Yes.'

'Then do as I say. Take care, my dear.'

The telephone woke me abruptly from a deep sleep. I'd have had to make such an effort to get to it ... Suddenly it all came back to me, and I felt a terrible pain in my stomach.

'You make too much of it, child ...'

Yes, but he'd promised ... I went back to sleep. I dreamed I was in a big room full of people, all I could see was their faces. I didn't know any of them. Suddenly all these faces began to laugh, and they all turned into my father's face, they were laughing so hard that someone I couldn't see began to bang on something that I couldn't see either. I woke up with a beating heart; someone was banging on my door very loudly.

'Open the door, child, I know you're there. Come on, open up!'

I opened the door to Sartre, and turned my back on him.

'I know what you're feeling, child ...'

'Don't come near me, don't touch me, I don't want to hear anything, you've cheated me, I shall never be able to forgive you, I don't trust you any more, do you understand?'

I dragged myself over to my bed. Sartre followed me.

'You promised, but you did it and you presented me with a *fait accompli*.'

'I know, but you know very well that you'd never have given your consent ...'

'You shouldn't have promised, that's all.'

I burst into tears.

67

'Listen to me, child, I'd have liked to prepare you, to explain that it doesn't count for me, and especially to tell you myself. I understand what you're feeling . . .'

'No, you can't understand.'

'I'll make up for it, believe me.'

'You and your making up, you can stuff it! You can never make up for such treachery, never! And don't call me "child"! Right now, you can go away, I don't want to hear any more and you won't get another word out of me.'

No words could express the remorse I feel when I think back to how much I hurt Sartre that day.

I refused to see him for several weeks. Castor phoned me.

'At least give him a chance to explain how it all came about.'

In the end, I gave in. Sartre tried to explain to me that he had been dealing with the most urgent things. And that Lena's arrival had caused a scene with Arlette.

It took him years to persuade me. Five years later, Sartre happily suggested that we both sign the following contract:

> We, the undersigned, Jean-Paul Sartre, known as Poulou, and Liliane Siegel, known as the Bastard, hereby decide that the twelve months beginning 1st December 70 and ending 1st December 71 will be a continuous 'pleasure object' for both of them. This contract will be subject to renewal by tacit agreement in December 71 unless Liliane Siegel terminates it. In witness whereof we sign.
>
> Paris, 5.5.70.

10

It would be wrong to give the impression that my relationship with Sartre was confined to 'sessions', which were often painful but oh so salutary.

Sartre struck a good balance. He deliberately waited for what he considered an opportune moment before bringing up certain questions, and it was always when we had several hours to spend together; our breakfasts were not suitable, both because of the place and the shortage of time.

Sartre talked about himself, about what he had done the previous day. He advised me on my reading, urged me to see certain films and plays, sometimes took me to an exhibition, encouraged me in my work. He took a full part in the education of my son, whom he saw alone once a week from the age of nine onwards; he consoled me when I had troubles of all sorts; he organized my holidays in detail and paid for them when they were too expensive.

Sartre helped me to discover and enjoy books of history, detective stories, Russian, American and Italian literature, Proust and caviar, good food and wine. He bought me records to encourage my liking for music, which was the only thing that my father, in spite of himself, had passed on to me at birth.

On his advice, I bought a piano on credit and took

lessons. Sartre was strict and demanding; he said he would check on my progress when the time came.

He waited about a year, and then decided that he would come to my place and hear me play.

The following Tuesday he came, sat down in an armchair, put his hands on his thighs and waited without a word. He looked so solemn that my hands began to tremble.

'Come on, child, I'm listening.'

Timidly, I began to play a Bach prelude which we had spoken about at length, and made a mistake.

'Go on, it doesn't matter.'

I finished it with difficulty. I had stopped trembling.

'Start again. It'll be all right this time.'

I began the prelude again at the beginning, forgetting Sartre, possessed by the music and the joy it gave me.

Sartre was sparing with compliments and detested flattery. But that day he really rewarded me.

'That's very good, child. You know how to appreciate a good wine and you will play the piano well. I'm pleased with you. You must carry on, and practise every day.'

Later, when I came out of clandestinity, Sartre often came to my place. He played the piano. He played it well. At his request I had bought some Chopin, Debussy, Satie. Often he would improvise, or we would play duets. There are no words to express what I felt then.

Since Sartre's death the piano has remained silent. I must start again one day ... Closed as it is, in shape, with its light-brown varnished wood, it looks too much like a coffin!

11

The events of May 1968, in which I participated very fully, had caused our conversations that often had the very precise aim of making me become more open to life, as Sartre put it, to become less fequent. One Tuesday afternoon at the end of June the weather was superb, but we were not in good spirits.

'Oh, I have no illusions. You'll see, child, the government will let a few days go by and then it'll open the floodgates, there'll be enough petrol for everyone, it's too good an opportunity to miss. People will go on holiday, holidays make them apathetic. Incidentally, we haven't planned anything for your holiday, have we?'

'No. You said, "We'll think about that when I come back from Yugoslavia," and then everything happened so quickly.'

Sartre became thoughtful, remained silent for a long moment, and then said with an amused look, 'What would you say to a trip to Rome? You'll take a sleeper, I'll put you in a little hotel I know well, I won't be able to see you as much as you would like, but . . .'

'To Rome?'

'Why not? I'll work out your programme for you, and you'll see where we're staying, Castor and I. Do you like the idea? I'll give you some *sous*, of course.'

I couldn't keep back my tears.

'That's the way I get thanked! If you start crying, you little idiot . . .'

'It's so unexpected!'

'But the thing is, I'm leaving with Arlette in a few days for Yugoslavia! You see to your train ticket, I'll ask Castor to make the hotel booking, you can tell her what time you'll arrive, that'll be safer, I might lose it and then Arlette might find it. I'll come and meet you at the station. Don't miss your train!'

I arrived at the station with plenty of time to spare. The train was at the platform but the doors were closed. I found my carriage, put my suitcases down, and was gripped by a terrifying feeling of anguish. I felt as if I was in the middle of a thick fog, strange sounds of muffled bells were thumping in my ears, I clutched on to a man who was passing.

'Monsieur, I think I'm going to faint . . .'

'She must be pregnant, we must get a doctor, look how pale she is . . .'

The voice seemed very faint, but then it grew louder. I opened my eyes but immediately shut them again. Faces were studying me, I thought I was having a nightmare. A nasal voice announced names that didn't mean a thing to me and then suddenly:

'Take your seats, please.'

My train! My suitcase! I jumped up so quickly that the people recoiled. The clock said eight o'clock, I had plenty of time.

The people became insistent:

'Would you like us to call the police, you can't go like that . . .'

'I'm all right now, thank you, it must be the heat, I'll lie down on the train.'

The conductor came to my rescue. Seeing his uniform,

the people reported the incident to him and then reluctantly melted away. He asked me for my ticket and picked up my luggage.

'Come with me, I'll see you to your seat.'

Sartre had advised me to give him some *sous* and to book a seat for dinner. I slipped a note into his hand, thanked him, asked him to let down the bed and bring me some water as soon as possible.

'After the train has started. Thank you very much, Mademoiselle. Will you be all right?'

As I child, I had always had difficulty in falling asleep. I was huddled up against my sister Léa, to leave room for my other two sisters who slept at the foot of the same bed. The sound of the passing trains terrified me. We'd been in several air-raids. My parents slept in the room where we were hidden, opposite the station at Évreux.

'Have you still got your revolver?' (My mother was whispering, but I could hear her perfectly.) 'If you hear the little bell at the gate, kill the children first, then me and you, I don't want us to be separated, I'd rather we died right away, all together.'

The little bell rang and I woke up in a daze, covered in sweat.

'First service, first service.'

I looked at my watch, it was eight forty-five. Why so much noise? They must have put me over the wheels, I shall never be able to sleep. Although that's better than having nightmares!

'Here's your water, Mademoiselle. Would you like me to turn your bed down?'

A uniformed man was standing in front of me; I hadn't heard him come in. I nearly screamed, but merely went out into the corridor. The conductor said a few words which were lost in the din of a train that suddenly rushed past in the opposite direction. I stared fixedly at the carpet in my compartment. I went in, shut and bolted the door. I looked at the white sheets. Outside, night was falling. I started to undress. Irresistibly, my eyes went from the carpet to the white sheets. I lay down on the couchette. The rhythmic sound of the train grew louder, became unbearable. With my head under the pillow the sound that reached me was muffled, but metrical: carpet – white sheets – carpet – white sheets.

> I was standing by the telephone, I was waiting for news of my mother, she'd promised to phone me.
>   'Hallo, Maman, hallo?'
>   'Yes, it's me.'
>   'Where are you?'
>   'In Spain.'
>   'How are you, did you have a good journey?'
>   'A bit long, but can you imagine, there was a carpet and white sheets in the train!'

I shivered. Was I too leaving on my last journey? Poor Maman, how many times had I heard her say:

> 'She went off in a train and she didn't come back. You can't say that to a mother, you understand. She must come back, she will come back, she's alive, I'm sure she is, she's lost her memory, she's forgotten her name, but she knows I'm waiting for her. One day the postman will bring a letter, you'll see.'

For fifteen years she watched for the postman, then she gave up and I knew she was going to die. What was she thinking about in that train which she was taking for the first time?

A long, grating sound awoke me suddenly, I was blinded by the daylight. I got up at once, and looked at my watch. It was seven o'clock. A few more hours and I would be with Sartre in Rome.

As we arrived, I leaned out of the window on the platform side. But how was I going to find him in the midst of all those people?

'Get out of the train and wait for me, child, do you hear me? I shall find you, but whatever you do, don't move. I shall be there, you can rely on that.'

The train was still moving slowly. I searched the crowd with my eyes, and saw him. I was going to shout his name to attract his attention but one doesn't shout 'Sartre' on a station platform! Imagining the scene, I burst out laughing, and then Sartre saw me in his turn.

'That's a nice way to show your joy, child,' he said, as he took my luggage.

It was suffocatingly hot in the taxi that took us to the Piazza della Rotonda, by the Pantheon.

'Did you have a good journey?'

'*Oh là là*!' (I wasn't going to tell him . . .)

We went up the few steps to the lobby of the Hotel Senato. A young man carried the luggage. Another, rather older, greeted Sartre cordially, and then very courteously wished me a pleasant stay in Rome. I still hadn't taken in the fact that I was in Rome. I was very moved, and turned to Sartre.

'Come on, child, are you dreaming? They're waiting to show you your room.'

'Yes, that's exactly it: I'm dreaming.'

Sartre laughed heartily.

'Go on up, I'll wait for you. You'll see, it isn't luxurious but it's quiet and comfortable. I've been here before you, you know. After that, if you aren't too tired, we'll go and have lunch in the Piazza Navona.'

We walked slowly along the street. Sartre was holding my arm. Every so often we passed a Gentleman who raised his hat, bowed and said: '*Buon giorno.*' Sartre replied politely.

'Are they going to interrupt us like that all the time?'

'They're more discreet than in France; they greet you and pass on.'

Sartre had reserved a table on a restaurant terrace in the Piazza Navona.

'You sit there, you'll be able to see it better.'

'I can't talk and look at the same time, but I want to do both at once!'

'You can see the square as much as you like, it's very close to your hotel.'

Sartre translated the menu for me in its entirety. Then he ordered some wine. The waiter brought a thick glass carafe containing a yellowish, rather cloudy liquid which I looked at suspiciously.

'Taste it, you must.'

I drank a little.

'It's revolting, it tastes musty.'

'It's always like that at first, it's a local wine. I like drinking it in Rome. Eat, child, pasta has to be eaten hot.'

I was staring at the fountain.

'Well, child, what are you thinking about?'

'The sound of water is soothing, I was wondering why.'

'It's time to go, child, I have to work now.'

At their hotel, Castor was sitting on the terrace. Her

headscarf and her light blouse intensified the colour of her eyes. She stood up. She was radiant.

'Hallo, how are you? How was the journey? It's awful by train, it's too long. You ought to think about going back by air. Is the hotel all right?'

'But my dear Castor, she's only just arrived, don't talk about her going back! We had lunch at Maestro Stefano's.'

'What did you have to eat?'

I looked at them tenderly. Was it their summer clothes – Sartre had taken off his jacket and was wearing a natural-coloured, short-sleeved sports shirt – or was it because I was seeing them together for the first time in a different place? The place about which Sartre had said to me:

> 'It's in Rome with Castor that I'm really happy. I have no restrictions, just two phone calls to make in the evening.'

'It's lovely, isn't it? We have a magnificent view! Do sit down, you must be exhausted. What would you like to drink? We've worked out a programme for you – where have you put it?' (She was addressing Sartre.) 'Naturally you must organize things in your own way, but I would advise you to visit the Forum and the Coliseum in the early morning; in the afternoon the heat is unbearable.'

I looked at Castor as if I were seeing her for the first time. I was too moved to speak.

'You must go, child. Are you sure you can find your hotel? I'll ring you at eight this evening and we'll have breakfast together tomorrow.'

I was relieved. I needed to be alone. I wanted to take refuge in this newfound happiness which it seemed impossible to share. I walked slowly back to my hotel and lay down on the bed. No, I wasn't dreaming. It was summer, I was in Rome, I was going to see Sartre again tomorrow, Castor had welcomed me warmly, I no longer felt excluded and I realized how frustrated I had been for the past eight years.

I have never been back to Rome after Sartre's death. Everything is still intact in my memory: the squares, the streets, the monuments, the fountains, the cemeteries, the cafés, the restaurants, the museums.

Advised by Castor or by Sartre, alone or with him, I traversed Rome in a frenzy. When I saw Sartre the time was never long enough, I had so many things to tell him and to ask him.

When I said goodbye to Castor at the hotel I was in a terrible state; I had forgotten all about the train journey. Sartre was getting impatient.

'Child, the taxi's waiting for us!'

'Castor, could you let me have a sleeping-pill?'

'Of course. It's essential for such a long journey!'

Sartre came with me into the carriage, took my hands in his and said in astonishment, 'How can anyone have freezing-cold hands in this heat?'

'Er . . .'

'I understand, I always feel gloomy when I leave Rome. I console myself by thinking that I shall come back. You too, will come back, child, that's a promise!'

12

When I saw Sartre again after my stay, he scrutinized my face as usual, observed that I was 'in rather a good state', and suggested that we should tidy up the books. It was a superb day, and Sartre's proposition struck me as an encouraging sign: we weren't going to talk about me. For several months he had been convinced that I was being obstinate when I declared that I couldn't remember my early childhood. He regretted it for me, we were so close to the goal . . . Nevertheless, he had voluntarily let go.

We always proceeded in the same way with the books, by collecting up all the Pléiade editions scattered around. Sartre possessed them all: Gallimard sent them to him as they were published. He was extremely attached to them, and so far as I know never lent them to anyone, although he gave away a lot of other books.

I dusted the shelves and the books, then handed them to Sartre, who arranged them in alphabetical order.

As I was handing a book up to him Sartre stared at my right hand and said in amazement, 'Where does that scar come from? It doesn't look very . . .'

'That! That's the most wonderful memory of my life! I remember it very well, even though I was only at nursery school!'

I told Sartre in great detail the circumstances in which

my mother had slammed the door of the van my father was driving on my hand, how she had taken me to hospital where they X-rayed it and put on a very big bandage, which I was very proud of, but above all how she had looked after me then, only me, and made a big fuss of me.

Sartre was probably astonished at these unexpected discoveries but he didn't show it. Thanks to his skill, his intentional silences, his guarded pressures, it was that very day that he got me to understand, and accept, that one could repress one's past, that that was where the real causes of my trouble lay, and that I must try to dig them up in order to destroy them. He explained that I ought to go to an analyst, I needed a professional, someone who was neutral, obviously not just anyone, to finish off the 'work' begun by him eight years before, and that my salvation depended on it. He had a lot of trouble persuading me that my suspicions were unfounded.

'Are you trying to get rid of me?'

Nevertheless, he declared in solemn tones that he would break with me once and for all if I ever took it into my head to stop the therapy without consulting him.

Twelve months later I phoned Sartre at six in the afternoon. It was a Friday and he was working with Castor; he was not to be disturbed there unless something exceptional had happened, and of course it was he who made that decision . . .

'I've finished my therapy.'

Five minutes later he joined me at the Raspail-Vert.

'You look cross.'

'I'm very cross. I warned you, though . . .'

'Listen, I know what it was you sent me to the analyst to find out. I was convinced that I wasn't loved when I was very little. I kept begging for proof but I couldn't believe it. Obviously I'd got everything mixed up. Basically, since I hadn't been loved I wasn't lovable, so no one loved me. No one can understand this better than you. Do you follow me?'

'Perfectly, but . . .'

'In actual fact, I've discovered that I was my mother's favourite daughter until my last little sister was born. After that, things changed, there was the war, and Pauline died. You know what happened next: the separation, the clandestinity, and Bella's deportation. No question of love any more! Fear predominated, the only aim was survival. Believe it or not, my mother said to me: "You're so beautiful, so intelligent, one day you'll marry a prince." '

'She meant a rich man, the poor woman! Who told you that?'

'I remembered it, and I checked with Fanny. She told me that I was adulated, they got me to sing in Yiddish when I was three, and a whole lot of things came back to me. I remember that they used to stand me on a table and I'd imitate the accent of a Romanian aunt I was very fond of, everyone clapped, you know the kind of damn stupid things they get children to do . . . but which are all part of life . . .'

'But the decision to stop the therapy . . .'

'The reconciliation with my mother. Did you know that? That was what I had to achieve, it seems. It's true that I feel perfectly able to visit her grave, now.'

'That isn't necessary any more.'

'Since yesterday, such a lot of things have happened inside me! It's very odd, it felt as if it was physical, as if I'd suddenly been emptied and then completely filled again in a different way . . .'

'But you disobeyed . . .'

'I disobeyed my "Mother-Sartre", knowing that there

was a real danger of my being cut off, and I wasn't afraid. Doesn't that prove that I'm beginning to grow up?'

Sartre was looking at me with an expression I'd never seen before.

'There's a strange expression on your face. You look very proud of yourself, as if you'd made me, and made me very well.'

'There's some truth in what you say, child . . .'

I walked back with Sartre to his place. He turned round behind the glass door and waved.

One day I must bring myself to tell him how much I love him!

That year for the first time, in spite of his absence I had a wonderful holiday. I described it to him, and was well rewarded:

8 August [1969]

My little darling,

That, I think, is the first happy – completely happy – letter you have ever written me. It gave me real pleasure. I hope you'll keep it up in Zermatt. There's something really satisfying, *even for other people*, about a girl breathing contentment from every pore. I tell you, people who are unhappy ought to keep quiet about it. But there's no harm in showing that you're contented. Carry on, swamp me in satisfied letters. I shall never get tired of them. No, you aren't having a fit of vanity, that would be quite different: it's more that you're acquiring the inner contentment of people who were happy in their cradle, which after all you were, although you were cheated of it later. If X is 'very loving', I'm sure he senses the inner embellishment in you. And I'm very touched that you thought tenderly of me while I was with Arlette.

Dubrovnik is a pleasant town, very old with stone streets which look like porcelain, they've been made so shiny by the inhabitants' feet. Nothing to report. At the moment I'm in Rome with Castor. We spent a few days in Florence. At the moment, we're working. It's the *afa** all over Italy: 33 to 37 degrees in the shade and humidity in the air. Rome is still red and beautiful, but above it the sky is white (haze rather than clouds). People are suffering from the heat. Even the Italians. So are we. Out of doors. But indoors, in the place you know, we still have air-conditioning, with its cicada sound, and we work in comfort.

My darling, my bastard, I'll write to you again: to Paris, around 15 August. Be gay, keep your tender feelings for me . . .

With much love,

J.-P. Sartre

* Italian for the dog-days.

III

13

In her memoirs, Simone de Beauvoir has described the principal events in Sartre's life after he decided to help the Maoist movements, in particular the Proletarian Left (*La Gauche prolétarienne*). So I will confine myself to giving an account of certain decisive facts in my 'militant' career with Sartre and the GP.

When Le Bris and Le Dantec were arrested, convicted and imprisoned, Sartre took on the editorship of the paper *La Cause du peuple (The People's Cause)*.

More and more in demand by the Maoists, Sartre had no intention of allowing his meetings with them to cut into his working time. He gave them an appointment in 'my time', and told me with great joy that he was going to 'introduce me officially into his life'. Sartre was very proud of this brainwave. From then on I would be able to visit him openly, and greet him in the street. The Maoists didn't call anyone *vous*, so I would no longer have to be afraid that the revealing *tu* might escape me. I would learn a lot, and I'd be able to do heaps of things with him openly and publicly.

'You see, child, as from this second you're no longer clandestine, you've been promoted a militant in the *Gauche prolétarienne* think-tank.'

I threw my arms round Sartre's neck, which quite surprised him.

'This isn't a joke?'

'Of course it isn't. In a few minutes I shall introduce you to the "chief", whom you're supposed to have known for a long time.'

And that was how I happily got to know Pierre Victor, alias Benny Lévy, whom I took to from our first meeting, probably because he was the one Sartre was the most interested in, because he was a Jew and clandestine, but above all because he was responsible for my life in the open.

I came out of my clandestinity and immediately became the secretarial department of a clandestine movement. As the administrative proceedings would have taken too much of his time, Sartre bestowed on me the official title of co-editor of the paper. I didn't share all the opinions of the GP, far from it, but this was a chance to do something for Sartre and chiefly, as I realized later, to make up for what Sartre called 'my bastardy'.

Sartre bitterly regretted it afterwards. And in fact, I took it very badly when I was later twice accused and convicted of libelling Raymond Marcellin. Coming out of the law courts, Sartre said to me, 'My poor child, I wanted to associate your name with mine, I thought it was a good thing for you. I behaved like a bloody fool.'

Everything concerning the Maoists' relations with Sartre had to come through me. For Sartre, I was the link and the barrier. I fulfilled my new task scrupulously, greedily savouring the name of Sartre being associated with mine at every step; it opened all doors to me!

La Cause du peuple was not banned, but its anonymous sellers were arrested, sentenced and imprisoned. The authorities even went so far as to arrest anyone found in possession of a copy. A decision had to be made: a way must be found to circumvent these scandalous hypocrisies.

That was the origin of the idea of asking well-known people to sell *La Cause du peuple* in the street: I was given a list of about sixty names that included men and women writers, film-makers, actors and actresses, journalists and scientists. I was transformed, but Sartre wasn't taken in.

'All this is just "social", but you were devalued by the social, and you will be revalued by the social. Well, it's done, and from now on you're going to live in broad daylight. You see, child, it's possible to be a bastard but still recognized!'

I began to phone the people on the list and invited them to meet in my flat, which contained a very large room without any furniture which I used for my yoga classes.

'Hallo, may I speak to François Truffaut, please?'

'Who's calling?'

'Jean-Paul Sartre.'

'Hold on, please.'

The meeting took place on a Saturday afternoon. Castor and Sartre were the first to arrive, punctual as usual, and they came and sat down in my yoga room. Then about forty people turned up in less than half an hour. It was an unusual sight; they all gave their names as they came in, and I gave mine. The only things missing were the *petits fours* and champagne. Things became lively. Very soon, little groups began to form. The Maoists spoke of their past and future exploits, the film-makers of the cinema, the actors (or rather the actresses, because no actors came that day) of censorship.

Marguerite Duras explained to Sartre that she couldn't tolerate crowds, so it was no use counting on her. At that moment Sartre closed up. Castor looked at the people in amazement. She looked at Sartre and at her watch at the same time, and then went over to Sartre.

'We're wasting our time. We must come to a decision.'

'I agree.'

Barely concealing her irritation, Castor took the floor firmly, imposing a sudden silence.

'We've been here for more than an hour. You all know what our plan is: to sell *La Cause du peuple* in the street. All those in agreement, raise your hands.'

The result was dismaying: eight hands were raised, including those of Castor and Sartre. All the others justified themselves by having previous engagements; it would be for another time.

'Right. Let's go.'

A Maoist took the floor.

'Just a minute. Before we go, we need one or two cars to take *La Cause du peuple*. Liliane's and her son's are permanently tailed by the security branch.'

Everyone looked at everyone else, like schoolchildren when the headmaster is waiting for someone to own up; it was comic. A few gazes, among them Sartre's, alighted on Marguerite Duras, who immediately retorted to Sartre: 'Ask me for anything you like but my car: it's what I hold most dear!'

Sartre, who was quick at repartee, remained dumb. His face hardened, and then he gave the ghost of a smile. For anyone who knew him it was crystal clear: at that moment Marguerite Duras had ceased to exist for him; it was irreversible. Suddenly, everyone poured out on to the stairs, which reverberated with an indescribable racket; footsteps resounded noisily, voices were raised, perhaps out of necessity, but probably because they were relieved at having finally got away. Sartre was disappointed.

'They aren't prepared to go into action! By the way, child, wasn't Truffaut supposed to come?'

We were in the hall. I opened the street door and found myself face to face with François Truffaut.

'I'm so sorry I'm late, I was in the middle of sound-editing. What did you decide?'

'We're going to sell *La Cause du peuple* in the Avenue du Général Leclerc.'

'Fine. Let's go.'

Sartre greeted Truffaut warmly, and added, 'They've cleared out, there are just about ten of us. You had a lucky escape, it was unbearable!'

I watched them leave, a little disappointed. I had been given the job of getting in touch with the press immediately in the extreme case of the authorities daring to arrest one or other of the personalities in the street. I went back to my flat.

When Sartre came back, he told me that a cop had been just about to arrest him but had fled when someone shouted, 'You can't arrest a Nobel prize-winner!' This had especially delighted Truffaut.

Shortly afterwards Truffaut phoned me. He wanted to know what the position was. He explained that we needed to mobilize other personalities, that the same ones shouldn't always appear. He relied on me to explain to Sartre that he wasn't backing out, quite the contrary, that he was right behind us. He asked me to keep him informed. He was finishing a film and then had to go to the US for a few weeks, but as soon as I knew when the sellers of *La Cause du peuple* were to appear in court I was to let him know, and if need be he would put off his departure and come and give evidence. I was to give Sartre this assurance for him.

Sartre appreciated the acuteness of Truffaut's analysis

and asked me to chase up some personalities who hadn't taken part in the first sale.

Three days later, I went to the Coupole where François Truffaut was waiting for me. Ironically, he had asked me to have breakfast with him. I laughed, thinking that I was certainly destined to have breakfast with famous men.

When I went into the Coupole looking for Truffaut, he saw me first and came up to me.

'Why are you laughing? Is it the sun that makes you so gay?'

'It's a long story, I'll tell you later . . .'

'No, no . . .'

'You wouldn't understand. Your speciality is making films, isn't it? Mine is having breakfast with famous men, with two at any rate . . .'

'I imagine you're referring to Jean-Paul Sartre. If so, I'm most honoured.'

As I sat down at his table I took the time to observe him. I've always been very susceptible to well-dressed men. He was wearing a light-grey alpaca suit over a shirt of an indefinable blue, a Provençal sky tinged with lavender. His tie was in subtle harmony with the rest of his outfit and cut a striking line through all this blue. 'I really don't like ties,' I thought.

François Truffaut observed me in silence. I was wondering which of us was going to decide to speak.

'You're a cross between Paulette Goddard and Elizabeth Taylor. Yes, yes, if we change your hair-style it's Paulette Goddard. Though perhaps not the mouth . . .'

'*Oh là là*! It's a good thing I'm not an actress coming to see you for a part!'

François Truffaut laughed heartily. His eyes became mischievous.

'No, no, I should never have behaved like that! What would you like to drink? Or to eat, perhaps?'

'A coffee, please.'

'I didn't mean to embarrass you.'

'I'm not embarrassed, I'm intrigued.'

I was struck by his gaze: his eyes scrutinized, questioned, and appraised all at once, and at the same time gave the impression of being fixed on a detail.

'It's to do with your eyebrows . . .'

'What are you talking about?'

'You're staring at my mouth, I can stare at your eyebrows! Actually, I was wondering if, like Sartre, this way of searching a face determined your opinion. But perhaps it's professional conditioning?'

'I'm sorry.'

There was a long silence.

Then Truffaut added, 'I'm not staring at your mouth. Don't take any notice, I can't manage to be entirely with you. If it hadn't been for Jean-Paul Sartre, I wouldn't have come. I've withdrawn from everything; apart from my daughters and Madeleine, their mother, I hardly see anyone. I need to rebuild my life. I don't want you to think I'm rude, that's why I'm telling you this. Keep it to yourself. Have you ever had a really unhappy love affair?' Forgive me for being indiscreet.'

'I'm in the middle of one.'

'I'm sorry.'

'I'd have preferred us to have something else in common, something less painful. Don't be sorry, I think I know what you feel. You can rely on me to keep it to myself, I know how things get distorted by other people. Believe me, I've discovered that to my cost.'

'I don't know anything about you. I'm a public man, you know things about me, that's not fair.'

So I told him about the war, and my childhood as a little Jewish girl. The conversation very soon took on an unforeseen, almost intimate complexion.

'In short,' said Truffaut, 'we have three things in common: we both had a difficult childhood, we're in the middle of an unhappy love affair, and we have a passion for Sartre. We're a long way from the Maoists, aren't we?'

I was staggered. I'd come here to keep him informed about the action that was going to be taken concerning *La Cause du peuple*, and in less than two hours we had practically told each other everything, as he was to point out to me later.

A long time before I got to know François Truffaut I already felt close to his sensibility. I had seen all his films. *The Mischief Makers* had filled me with wonder, and left me with the image of the greedy but chaste eyes through which a man looks at a woman, and also of the beauty – and precarity – of a love story. *Les Quatres Cents Coups* made me disgusted with parents who don't know how to love their child, and with the solitude the child may endure.

In *Jules and Jim*, I felt as if I were in a dream. I was totally won over, even though at the time I wasn't yet capable of understanding that people could love each other in that way. The first time I saw *Jules and Jim*, towards the middle of the film I wondered how Truffaut would be able to end the story. I remembered *The Mischief Makers*, and I thought, 'Of course, death will separate them.'

I loved feeling that I was in the landscapes he shot in black and white: the country in *The Mischief Makers*, the mountains in *Jules and Jim*. If these films had been in colour, the magic wouldn't have worked. This was a period of my life when skies had to be grey.

Before we parted that morning, François confirmed his imminent departure for the United States. He would write to me. I promised to reply.

What passed between us that day gave rise to a friend-ship that lasted until his death.

14

When I got François's first letter, I wasn't surprised to discover what I had had a presentiment of: he described places in minute detail. What did strike me was that, just like Sartre, he described in detail the weather, the people he saw, and the state he was in. He invited me to write back, if I felt like it, and gave me even more details than Sartre did.

> Until 1st October, because letters take between four and six days, and I'm leaving for New York on the 6th. The exact address here is Beverly Hills Hotel 9641, Sunset Boulevard, Beverly Hills, 90210 California, US. After that, you can write to me in New York at the French Film Office, 745 Fifth Avenue, New York, NY 10022; I shall be there from 6th October until about the 15th.

I was to discover later that he had many affinities with Sartre, quite apart from his liking for precision.

Both preferred the company of women, and couldn't imagine having a tête-à-tête dinner with a man, made lasting friendships, which as a general rule they didn't mix, distinctly preferring twosomes, and finally were infinitely courteous.

On one precise point they behaved in a radically opposed fashion: Truffaut kept and carefully filed his correspondence and, more generally, everything concerning his work. Sartre attached no particular importance to such things, and often let himself be divested of his manuscripts.

I shall never forget the way François looked through a large section of the draft of *The Family Idiot* that I showed him one evening when he came to dinner with me. He caressed each page, from time to time saying in his inimitable fashion, 'Incredible, yes, yes, incredible!'

But when I told him that I had found the huge bundle of papers he was looking at in the rubbish-bin, salvaged it (with Sartre looking on in amusement), and brought it home in a shopping-bag as I couldn't bear to throw it away, François exclaimed, 'But it's not possible, it's negligence!'

'No. He just doesn't give a damn, that's all! He gives everything away, or almost everything, because no one must dare to touch his books, as you know.'

François too was very generous, but he liked his gifts to have concrete results. He almost reproached Sartre and Castor for their generosity.

'But François, Sartre and Castor have helped and are helping heaps of people by giving them the means to study for a degree, for instance. That's concrete, isn't it?'

'Yes, yes, but I don't like the idea of them keeping women without trying to get them to make something of their lives . . .'

'Castor doesn't do that, she's very particular and very vigilant, and Sartre did try, you know. He wrote plays for Wanda with fabulous parts, Michelle used to do translations and type his manuscripts, and as for Arlette, he wanted her to go on studying, but nothing came of it . . .'

'It's true that women are more vigilant. I'm glad to

hear Castor is like that. You know how much I respect
Sartre. Even so, I don't think there's anything very positive about keeping women who become totally dependent. I like the idea, yes, yes, of helping people to do
something that leads somewhere. But it's quite incredible
to think that he now hasn't got a bean, and ... there's
something there that I fail to understand.'

'He never stops saying, "When you start something,
you must go through with it." I think it's more complicated, though. He's terribly worried because he hasn't
any money, to the point where he wouldn't even let me
buy him a pair of trousers that he really needs, but do
you know what he did with the five thousand francs I
borrowed from you for him? He gave it to Contat! I was
supposed to pay it back to my brother, who lent it to him
for ...'

'To Contat! But he earns his living!'

'Of course he earns his living. We had a terrible scene.'

'You've been taken for a ride. Why did you give
him five thousand francs? And how are we going
to give that money back to my brother and François now? That's ten thousand francs!' (I was
beside myself.)

'He asked me for it.'

'You should have told him you didn't have it.'

'But I did have it. He didn't take me for a ride
because I agreed to it!'

'You're talking nonsense.'

'Forget it, child, it's my business. You're getting
on my nerves, you just don't understand!'

'That's the best yet! You ask me to borrow five
thousand francs from my brother because Hélène
has blown a fortune on goodness knows what,

then you send me to get it from François to pay my brother back, and you dare to tell me it's your business, and give me hell into the bargain! What do I tell my brother?'

'You tell him that he'll have it tomorrow!'

'But where will you get it?'

'I'll manage somehow.'

He didn't say any more for a long time, my anger subsided, and I regretted having flown off the handle. I felt sorry for him.

Then he said, 'I'll ask Castor.'

'I told you it was complicated! But in this case, it wasn't a woman.'

'At the beginning it was, though, if the money was for a certain Hélène.'

'That's true, but you don't know Hélène's story, which is incredible, as you say.'

One Tuesday afternoon I arrive at Sartre's as I do every Tuesday. He's full of beans, and he tells me:

'I've got news!'

'Well, it can't be anything dreadful, you look too cheerful. It's probably a woman!'

'Yes, a woman, but really, I had nothing to do with it – well, in a manner of speaking! Yesterday there's a ring at the door, I open it and there's a young woman standing looking at me and she says, "Do you remember me? We met in Athens at one of your lectures. I vowed to myself that I'd see you again, and here I am!" '

'So you're going to saddle yourself with yet another woman. I presume she's beautiful?'

'And why not? Talk about beautiful! I looked through the spy-hole before I opened the door.'

'It distorts everything . . .'

'Even so!'

François was fascinated by this new story and pressed me for more.

'After several return trips between France and Greece, Sartre suggested that she should come to live in Paris for a year, assured her that he'd look after her and help her to continue her studies. Sartre asked me to find her a flat, which I did, and of course he paid. Then I had to buy antique furniture, she didn't like modern stuff, and then a bed, linen, everything!'

François laughed heartily.

'I knew you'd like this story. That must be why I haven't told you before.'

'You did tell me that he went to Greece with Castor, I think . . . Was he in love with her?'

'I wouldn't say that. He liked her, she flattered him, it sickened me, in fact, but he wasn't taken in . . .'

'I can understand that, yes, yes. When you're old, you pay.'

'Will you do that, when you're old?'

'Why not? It seems fair to me.'

'In any case, he went off her just as quickly as he had taken to her, from one day to the next. She went back to Athens, taking all the furniture with her on the boat, at Sartre's expense.'

'It's a fine story, with a beginning, a middle and an end, the way I like them.'

15

In 1970 the *Gauche prolétarienne* unwittingly gave me two superb gifts: my officialization in Sartre's life, and a friendship of rare quality with François Truffaut which lasted for fourteen years. I would eventually have come out of my clandestinity in one way or another, Sartre would have found some pretext, but I would never have met François.

The state in which we both were, the one trying to rebuild his life, the other trying to accept the evidence of a break-up, might have alienated us. But it was quite the opposite, and this determined our relationship. From one point of view we were available, unattached, and we both earnestly wished to remain that way. François already had enormous respect for Sartre, but what interested him in what I told him was not the fact that I was close to Sartre, but 'the new light', as he put it, in which he saw Sartre through his relationship with me.

François was terrified of indiscretions. We made a pact: we would keep our mutual confidences to ourselves, and ourselves alone.

During the whole time that François lived at the Hotel George-V, a little over a year, we saw each other two evenings a week. We used to talk for hours. He liked straight talking, but wasn't averse to keeping certain facts hidden. When I pointed this out to him he smiled mischievously and complimented me. I refused his compliments and launched into interminable explanations. Sometimes they exhausted him, and he asked me to go.

'I haven't your talent for introspection!'

'It took me a long time to learn not to fake myself, you know! Well – as little as possible.'

'Fake yourself! What a lovely expression!'

'It's Sartre's.'

'With your permission, I shall make it mine!'

François did rebuild his life, he began to make films again. He phoned me, wrote to me. We saw each other regularly whenever his timetable permitted. He was less available, but still present. He was as considerate as I imagined only a woman could be, because she knows exactly with what kind of consideration she would like to be treated.

Whenever I went away, flowers would be waiting to welcome me home. Wherever he was, he never forgot a birthday, Christmas or the New Year.

If I had a sore throat or flu, a humorous little note would accompany a gigantic bouquet that wouldn't fit in the lift, so the delivery boy had to walk up the four flights.

He was in Los Angeles when he read in the press that Sartre had become nearly blind. He phoned me at three in the morning, excusing himself for waking me but he couldn't wait, he wanted to know how Sartre was, whether the terrible news was true, and how Sartre was reacting.

Later, when Sartre wanted him to produce ten television programmes on the history of twentieth-century France, he asked me to go with him. This was an unforgettable moment. I listened to them, I watched them. Sartre explained his plan in minute detail. François, listening carefully, acquiesced. 'Yes, yes, wonderful!'

Sartre was really disappointed when François told him that he couldn't consider committing himself to any project for more than a year; nevertheless he thought it a wonderful idea, the programmes must be made, they would constitute a unique document. He advised Sartre to get in touch with Roger Louis and Claude de Givray to produce the series, and he assured him that he would be at his entire disposal, that it would be a pleasure for him to help with the editing.

During the following months François was absorbed in the preparations for *Adèle H.*, but he always found a moment to enquire after the progress of the project. He was glad to think, from what I told him, that Sartre was beginning to recover his interest in work, and hence in life. François went off to Guernsey for the shooting, and made me promise to keep him informed of how things were going.

My dear Liliane,

Thank you for your letter and for the synopses of the programmes. The texts are indeed remarkably logical and clear, although there is not yet any indication of the visual and spoken presentation of this intellectual material. It's to be hoped that the two directors will not be unequal to the initial idea.

This may surprise you, but reading these texts chronologically made me feel demoralized and perhaps even apathetic.

They gave me the impression that the Right will always win in the end, and that although the idea of justice may progress quickly, justice itself advances at a snail's pace. If you think of politics as being comparable to a play enacted on a stage, you get the impression that people like Sartre (although there aren't many like him) are in the auditorium among the spectators, inviting them to demand a different play. Then at a certain point they pretend to change the play, they replace Pétain by de Gaulle and then by Giscard, but the play remains the same. You'll tell me that that's a good reason not to vote any more but to engage in revolution. But aren't revolutionaries them- selves just spectators, perhaps more turbulent, chucking stink-bombs at the stage, but who aren't going to make Marcellin-Poniatowski lose any sleep? I imagine, and I hope, that my way of seeing things is too simplistic. (I'm even certain that it is, to the point of asking you not to talk to the interested parties in the same terms.) It will be a good thing if, thanks to the liberal image of his regency that Giscard wants to put over, Sartre's truths can reach almost all the French. There's absolutely no doubt that these pro- grammes will cause a stir.

Anyway, the quality of the project, its clarity and breadth, make me sorry not to be able to play a full part in it – because of my children's film – but I shall be really pleased to follow its progress through the main stages and if necessary help to preserve the rigour of the project.

When I told François that the contract had been cancelled, his first reaction was utter amazement. He had been kept abreast of all the ins and outs, but Sartre's reputation, the respect he had for him, and finally the quality of the project itself had made him certain that it would finally come to fruition. 'They won't dare, there'd be too much of a fuss!'

His second reaction was terrible anger. This was due to two feelings, both equally intense. 'It's barely camouflaged censorship – and at the same time underhand. They'll use the cost of the programmes as an excuse, and the French will swallow it; money, that's the only thing they'll remember. They're depriving history of an exceptional document made by an exceptional man, but they'll think it's in their interests. Although the worst thing, I believe, is that they're clipping Sartre's wings. He'll never put so much of himself into any real project again after this blow. He was so enthusiastic! At his age, and not being able to see, the group work was wonderful for him. Jullian ought to have resigned, then he'd have come out of it with some credit! You ought to persuade him – tell him I can find some Americans to finance the project. I'm sure I can, Sartre is a beacon in the USA, I've told you that before!'

Sartre didn't want to hear of it, even though François's proposition had touched him more than he cared to show. He had decided to call things off after reading Monsieur Jullian's letter of 5 August 1975, which he called deceitful, hypocritical, flattering.

The break took place at my flat. Monsieur Jullian, accompanied by J. D. Wolfromm (who was always present at every meeting although he never said a word), was ill at ease, and tried to explain all his difficulties to Sartre.

'There's absolutely no doubt, it's up to you, an exceptional man, and up to the work as you conceive it, a work that is also exceptional . . .'

Sartre let him muddle on.

'I thought of putting on a pilot programme.'

Monsieur Jullian seemed to be reading the famous letter whose content we already knew by heart. Sartre remained silent for a moment, but finally decided to speak.

'You know, I proved myself a long time ago. When I have a manuscript ready for my publisher, he doesn't ask me to submit a sample beforehand!'

He rested his hands on his thighs, and said, 'Well. I don't think we have any more to say to each other. You know the way!' To which there was no answer.

They disappeared down the long corridor between the sitting-room and the front door. No one saw them out that day!

Throughout the years of our friendship, François was my favourite interlocutor, my unique and total confidant. He gently nagged me to go on taking notes: 'You're living an exceptional relationship: one day you'll write about it, you must keep a diary.'

In each of his films there was a wink, a way of saying, 'I'm working, but you are there.' He wrote to me regularly, mindful of my joys, my sorrows, my worries. Even when he was away, he was always there.

Shooting ends at the end of May. After that I shan't budge and we'll be able to see each other without outside pressures. I want you to know that I'm as keen as you are to resume our heart-to-hearts, and that I have a thousand questions to ask you.

Thank you for your letter and the cheque. I haven't been in touch on account of production + lines to learn, etc. But in any case I wouldn't have forgotten your birthday, I've got it down in my diary. If you still owe me 2,000 francs, please accept it as a present, you know better than I do what you need and would like.

I hope your sad little note only reflected one moment in your trip, only one episode in your holiday, but obviously I can't be sure. Phone me as soon as you get back and come and have dinner at my place and tell me all about it.*

Come back soon, dear Liliane, we miss you (the we also applies to Émilienne, who will cook you all sorts of delicacies).
P.S. I'm not sure of your exact dates so I'm sending this letter to Paris. Call me back.

I liked his letters. Our telephone conversations sometimes lasted for hours, and we laughed a lot. Only one, very painful one, haunts me. It was to do with the article that appeared in *Le Nouvel Observateur*, signed by Sartre and Benny Lévy. He was furious, beside himself.

'How can you possibly have let that through? It's pure shit! Those aren't Sartre's words, that's crystal-clear! That superior tone Pierre Victor – well, Benny Lévy – adopts is intolerable! This is very serious, Liliane, it's unacceptable! This is going to be translated throughout the world! People will deduce that Sartre is finished, that's the only thing they'll remember. I told you that that was precisely where the danger lay. In Sartre's present state, with all his ups and downs, the danger, yes, yes, is that they'll get their hands on him when the opportunity arises, it's manipulation! I'm horrified, and it'll probably happen again. What does he think? What do your friends think? What does Castor think?'

The violence of François's remarks paralysed me. I had never imagined he could get so angry, and I began to cry.

* I had been ill, and was convalescing.

'Don't cry, Liliane, for goodness' sake! It's not you I'm angry with . . .'

If only I had managed to say something! I didn't get another chance to tell François the position I was in then. In his eyes, for the first time I had broken faith.

In *Adieux*, published in France in 1981 (and in England in 1984),* Simone de Beauvoir very clearly states what she thought:

> I read this conversation at last – it was signed by Sartre and Benny Lévy, Victor's real name – about a week before it was to appear. I was horrified. It had nothing to do with the 'plural thought' that Sartre had spoken of in *Obliques*. Victor did not express any of his own opinions directly; he made Sartre assume them while he, by virtue of who knows what revealed truth, played the part of district attorney. The tone in which he spoke to Sartre and his arrogant superiority utterly disgusted all the friends who saw the document before it was published. And like me, they were horrified by the nature of the statements extorted from Sartre . . . I let Sartre know the full extent of my disappointment. It surprised him. He had expected a certain amount of criticism, but not this radical opposition. I told him that the whole *Temps modernes* team was with me. But this only made him the more set on having the conversation published at once.
>
> How can one explain this 'abduction of an old man', as it was put by Olivier Todd (who for his

---

* See Simone de Beauvoir's *Adieux: A Farewell to Sartre*, Penguin Books, 1985.

part did not recoil from the abduction of a dead one)?

In a caustic portrait of Victor, also in *Adieux*, Simone de Beauvoir attempted an explanation of this 'abduction of an old man':

> Victor had been one of the leaders of the *Gauche prolétarienne* and he had retained the 'little boss's' state of mind – everything had to give way before him. He moved easily from one conviction to another, but always with the same obstinacy. From the ill-governed intensity of his various enthusiasms he derived certainties that he would not allow to be called into question. This gave his words a vigor that some people found stimulating, but writing calls for a critical attitude of mind that he did not possess, and if anyone did adopt this attitude with regard to anything he had written, he felt injured. From that time on, he and I no longer spoke to one another; I avoided encountering him in Sartre's apartment. It was an unpleasant situation. Up until then, Sartre's real friends had always been mine too. Victor was the only exception . . .

16

After this conversation with François, I thought back to the start of my relations with Pierre Victor.

I had heard a lot about him. He was said to be dictatorial, brusque, uncompromising and very arrogant. As one always does, I had tried to form a picture of him from these rumours. I was surprised to see a man of middle height, already threatened by baldness.

His smile struck me: a warm, attractive, candid smile. I was afterwards to discover that very few people were favoured with it. Later, some of the militants told me that he used to treat them very harshly and give orders in an imperious tone of voice, with a scowl. I couldn't bring myself to believe them. With me, he was quite different: thoughtful, considerate, he wanted me to like him. When we were together, I was on the right side – Sartre's side.

Between 1970 and 1972, the years when Sartre agreed to support the *Gauche prolétarienne*, I met Pierre Victor only occasionally, always in Sartre's presence and in clandestine fashion, which obviously gave him a certain prestige in my eyes.

At that time I was exulting in my new status, flattered at participating in these 'summit meetings', in the course of which I made the acquaintance of Serge July, André Glucksmann, Jean-Claude Vernier, and many others. This radical change in my life blinded me. Pierre Victor was loquacious and I had concluded that this was a sign of extraordinary intelligence. He dared to confront Sartre head on. This staggered me, I had so often dreamed of doing so!

Sartre was amused by what he called my exaggerations, and concluded, 'He's not stupid, and that's a fact!'

We used to meet in a flat lent by one of my girlfriends, a different one each time. These meetings were kept secret. The Maoists invited to join us were hand-picked, and only told at the last moment.

Sartre found this excessive and grotesque. 'They take themselves for Resistance-fighters!'

When Pierre Victor arrived late for one of these meetings, Sartre told him off, saying, 'If you'd been in the Resistance during the war and been late for a rendezvous, it would have been fatal for you. That's the difference between you and a real Resistance-fighter.'

I was amazed by Pierre Victor's reaction. His face turned pale, his gaze hardened, his smile was transformed into such a dreadful grin that I was scared. I saw very clearly that day that he always had to be in the right and that he took the slightest criticism as an affront.

Why didn't I draw the obvious conclusions at the time, then?

17

Between 1970 and 1973, Sartre was caught up in a whirl of activities that he sometimes felt were useless and boring. At other times, and particularly when he was consulted beforehand and he thought them sensible and necessary, he was pleased to take part in them. This was the case when he agreed to participate in a 'people's court' under the auspices of the *Secours rouge** at Lens on 12 December 1970. In *Adieux*,† Simone de Beauvoir writes:

> I described this trial in *All Said and Done*, but since Sartre attached a great deal of importance to it, I should like to return to the subject here. In February 1970 sixteen miners were killed and many others wounded by a firedamp explosion at Hénin-Liétard. Since the Houillères, the state-owned coal mines, were obviously responsible, some unidentified young men threw Molotov cocktails into the offices of the management in retaliation, causing a fire. Without the slightest hint of proof the police arrested four Maoists and two former convicts. They were to be tried on Monday, 14 December, and *Secours rouge* sum-

* An organization whose aim was to struggle against repression.
† See above, p. 108

moned a people's court for Saturday, the 12th, in the town hall of Lens.

To prepare for this session, on 2 December, Sartre went with Liliane Siegel to sound out the miners.

It was suggested, then, that Sartre should go to Bruay, to find out the miners' opinions for himself. He asked me whether I would like to go with him, and as any chance to be with him was heaven-sent, I ignored my train-phobia.

During the whole journey, Sartre didn't take his nose out of his detective story.

A pleasant young man met us at the station with a car. He took us to the house of a mining family the Maoists had told us a lot about.

The man was of imposing height, a former miner, a former Resistance-fighter; he was jovial. His wife seemed tiny in comparison. She was all smiles, self-effacing, and busied herself in the room where we all sat round an oilcloth-covered table. From time to time she disappeared into the adjoining room, which I imagined was the kitchen because of the smells that escaped from it every time she opened the door. The room was simply furnished; the house was clean.

The miner described his life to Sartre, who was mo-rosely drinking *vin ordinaire* and asking questions. I dipped my lips into the wine I was given and regretted that I hadn't thought to bring a few good bottles. Sartre's moroseness, I was sure, came from the thought of having to spend a whole evening with nothing but this wine to drink. Another, very talkative, man arrived, and then one or two young women came and helped the mistress of the house to lay the table. We were told that dinner was ready. We were assailed by a strong smell of hot oil. The woman put a dish of rabbit down in the middle of the table.

Sartre was allergic to rabbit. I winced, but Sartre seemed unmoved. More and more bottles of wine were produced. Sartre ate the food on his plate politely. He was breathing with difficulty, and was then overcome by a terrible fit of coughing. I was scared. It seemed as if he could hardly breathe. Everything stopped.

The woman said, 'Aren't you well? Would you like to lie down?'

I answered for him. I knew him too well, he would have said, 'No thank you, I'll be all right.'

They showed us to a room on the first floor; Sartre had difficulty in getting up the stairs. I helped him to prop himself up on the bed.

'I'm going to call a doctor, it's an attack of asthma.'

'Don't do that, child, we've caused these people enough trouble as it is. Give me a couple of Nembutals, I'll be all right,' he said, with some difficulty.

I opened the window wide in spite of the cold, and sat down beside him. He fell asleep. I didn't want to leave him but it was late, and the young man with the car was waiting to take me to the place where I was going to sleep, a few kilometres away.

The next morning I found Sartre sitting in front of a bowl of steaming coffee. He assured me that he was perfectly all right. The talkative man and the young man with the car joined us. There was a female photographer. We were taken to see the mining villages, the entrance to a disused pit, they commented on the slag heaps, and then the photographer asked Sartre and me to pose behind one of the gates, gripping the big iron bars and pressing our faces against them. We were going in for militant tourism! The young man drove us back to our hosts, whom Sartre thanked warmly, and tried to reassure about the previous day's incident.

'Don't worry, that sometimes happens to me when I eat chips!'

We got back into the young man's car and he told us that we had an appointment in Douai with Eugénie Camphin, the mother and wife of miners in the Resistance who had been shot by the Germans. Sartre was surprised; he hadn't been consulted. It was quite a long way, the landscape was sinister, and there was fog.

Sartre knew the lady. She had a beautiful, honest face softened by a superb head of white hair done up in a dignified bun. She was delighted to receive him, and he greeted her very warmly. They talked about the *Secours rouge*, of which she, like Sartre, was a founder member. The front door-bell rang. She got up and immediately came back followed by Serge July, whom we had had no news of for several weeks.

'So that was the secret!' Sartre exclaimed. He was finally enjoying himself.

July explained to Sartre that he had gone into hiding and that he was in the neighbourhood. They talked at length. The young man with the car drove us to the station. On the train a furious Sartre exclaimed:

'What with a "triumphalist" on the one hand and a phoney Resistance-fighter on the other, we're doing very well, my poor child! I really begin to wonder what the hell I came here for!'

He buried himself in his detective story again and didn't say another word. On the platform I tried to find out a bit more.

'Why is July a triumphalist?'

'I'll explain. Come on, let's go and have a drink.'

I never did find out why Sartre had favoured July with this sobriquet, but that was what he liked to call him.

18

From time to time a Maoist would come and interrupt our breakfast, bringing a message that there was a rendezvous which it was imperative for Sartre to keep.

Pierre Victor knew Sartre's timetable and his generosity, so it was easy for him to 'use' Sartre and distract him from his work. The facts he put forward to try to mobilize Sartre were always imprecise and exaggerated. But we only discovered this much later.

In this way, on 13 February 1971, 'they' led Sartre into a trap that could have cost him his life.

A militant of *Vive la Révolution*, Richard Deshayes, had been disfigured by a tear-gas grenade during a demonstration. *La Gauche prolétarienne* organized the occupation of the Sacré-Cœur basilica, hoping to bring off a 'coup' that would alert public opinion; they assured us they had the consent of Monseigneur Charles. The Maoists insisted to Sartre, 'If you're there, the press will come.'

When I went into the church with Sartre I was amazed to find no one there but a few elderly believers who were very obviously praying.

Sartre didn't understand, and asked a Maoist who was accompanying us: 'Where are the "peaceful" demonstrators? I thought there were supposed to be a lot of people here.'

'They're going to come in small groups, so as not to be spotted.'

'But the idea was to alert public opinion!'

Sartre leaned over and murmured to me: 'I've been taken for a ride again. It's a stupid gimmick.'

The church gradually filled up with young men. A priest came up to Sartre, who told him that he would like to speak to Monseigneur Charles. The priest told him politely that he would pass on his request, and then disappeared.

It seemed a long time to me. A Maoist came and told us that all the doors had been shut, with one exception. I began to panic. Suddenly, the church was invaded by the riot police, who began to hit out violently and indiscriminately. I felt myself being lifted off the ground and swept along to a corner of the church near the one door that was still open. I looked around desperately for Sartre. He was propped up against a wall near me, protected by two Maoists. The scene in the body of the church was appalling, people were screaming, the police were lashing out. I don't remember how we came to find ourselves in a nearby café. I was terrified.

A Maoist joined us, and told us that he had witnessed a veritable massacre and assured us there were some dead. He had seen with his own eyes some of the riot police impaling demonstrators on the iron railings surrounding the Sacré-Cœur. We were horrified.

The next morning the papers, according to their 'colour', tendentiously described the occupation of the basilica, but on one point they were all agreed: one person had been wounded but no one had been killed.

On 15 February, Sartre and Jean-Luc Godard gave a press conference about this affair which attracted a lot of attention. Three days later, Sartre resigned from the management committee of the *Secours rouge*. He told me that he would continue to take part in some of the demonstrations they organized, but that he refused to be held responsible for the stupid actions of the Maoists who had in fact infiltrated the *Secours rouge*. 'What's more, I don't like to be taken for a bloody fool!'

19

So many facts have been reported – embroidered to please some, distorted to suit others. So many people who only saw Sartre two or three times have claimed him as an old friend. The dead are no longer here to re-establish the truth. People talk, and talk!

In 1968, my son and I were members of an action committee in the 14th *arrondissement*. The committee met in a café. The manager took a dim view of us – some twenty people occupying his tables from eight in the evening until two in the morning and drinking very little. No one knew of our relations with Sartre.

A young man, who seemed well informed, took the floor and suggested, 'Let's ask Sartre for a flat; I know he owns at least five in the Montparnasse tower block.'

Amid the general enthusiasm, my son retorted, 'Where did you get that from? Do you take his suits to the cleaners for him?'

'What, for that poofter?' the young man flung at him.

'Have you had the honour of having him up your backside, you poor sod?'

'Who, me?'

'Not you, no, we know that, but a cousin of a cousin of your uncle. Never let me hear you say that again or I'll hang you on the curtains!'

More seriously, I have read in a chronology that is used for reference:

> March 1972, Sartre approves the kidnapping of Nogrette by the clandestine group *La Nouvelle Résistance Populaire.**

Sartre did not approve of this kidnapping. We heard of it together when we were reading the papers the same day. I was also with him when, forty-eight hours later, a Maoist turned up at his flat in a pitiful state and asked him, 'What can we do, do you think?'

'You should have asked me before!'

The same chronology states:

> 6 – 13 April [1975]. Stay in Portugal with Simone de Beauvoir and Paul Victor. Originally intended to be a private trip, Sartre's visit to Portugal takes on the character of a stay to gather political information . . .

In actual fact, this stay in Portugal with Simone de Beauvoir, her adopted daughter Sylvie Le Bon de Beauvoir, and Pierre Victor, had been meticulously planned. Pierre Victor was not sufficiently intimate with Sartre and Simone de Beauvoir to go on holiday with them. His presence alone vouches for the political nature of the trip, which also included Serge July.

Still in the same chronology:

> October [1973]: in the autumn, Pierre Victor, principal leader of the ex-*Gauche prolétarienne* (which he was responsible for dissolving) becomes Sartre's permanent collaborator . . . and

---

* Chronology by Michel Contat and Michel Rybalka, in *Œuvres romanesques*, Vol. I, Sartre, La Pléiade, Gallimard.

Victor reads aloud to Sartre the works he can no longer read for himself.

And further on:

From the autumn of 1973, they work together for three hours a day on their project *Pouvoir et Liberté* (Power and Freedom).

What distorted, noble terms these facts are presented in! One Tuesday at the end of May 1973, Arlette, with whom I had become friendly, my son and I had taken Sartre to consult an eye specialist. Out of discretion, Gérald and I waited for them in the street. It was a wonderful day. I was very worried, and had no illusions.

A few weeks before, Sartre, as he often did, was admiring the light, the blue of the sky, and he called me to come and look:

'You see all that lightning, child? Isn't it strange in a cloudless blue sky! Well, haven't you got anything to say? You must admit it's strange!'
'To tell you the truth, I didn't see it!'
'I saw it, I'm quite sure I did.'

When I got home I rushed to the phone and rang a woman friend who is an opthalmologist.

'I'm afraid Sartre has gone raving mad, he's certain he saw lightning in the middle of the afternoon, but there wasn't a cloud in the sky...'
'He hasn't gone mad, Liliane, he probably had a...'
'What does it mean, your ghastly word? Is it serious?'
'It could be.'

'Don't tell me such things. He can only see with one eye as it is!'

'Ah, here they are,' Gérald said.

'It isn't good news, my poor child. It seems that it's irreversible.'

That was Sartre's comment. Nothing worse could have happened to him, yet he insisted that we should all four go and have dinner in a restaurant.

Sartre knew that his life was going to collapse. I know, because he told me so in confidence later; he said he was already envisaging the changes his semi-blindness was going to bring about and the dependence it would entail, but he didn't let anything show. What a lesson he gave us that evening!

When he came back from Rome at the end of September, he greeted me very solemnly. That wasn't like him, and I was scared.

'Sit down, child, I've got something serious to say to you. Don't be afraid, it isn't against you – on the contrary. I'm going to entrust you with a mission, and I want you to get on with it right away. My sight is failing, and I can't see to read any more. Don't interrupt me, and behave yourself. There's no way I can write if I can't read what I've written. My dear Castor isn't young enough to read to me every morning, it would be too much of an imposition and too tiring for her. There's only one solution that I can see, and anyway, I like it: Pierre. I get on well with him, he's lively and intelligent. He'll have to come on Mondays, Wednesdays and Fridays from eleven to one. I'll give him some *sous*, that'll help his finances. Castor can work with me two mornings a week, and Arlette can take her turn when she sleeps here. On Sundays I'll make music while I'm waiting for you.' (This

123

was his way of saying that he'd listen to France-Musique.)

'Behave yourself,' Sartre had said. I knew perfectly well what that meant: don't indulge in any useless emotion, these are the facts, we have to find a solution, that's all. But I couldn't keep my tears back.

'Well, child, are you listening? Pierre likes you, you get on well with him. Talk to him, you must persuade him.'

'Why don't you ask him yourself?'

I had asked this stupid question to give myself time to pull myself together. But in actual fact I had just realized that Sartre hadn't noticed that I was crying, he hadn't seen my tears. He had so often said to me:

'Don't cry, child, not like that!'

From then on I could cry in silence. I was devastated, but I immediately added, 'There are moments when I tell myself that you've been wasting your time with me! Of course I'll talk to him, and I'm quite sure that he won't hesitate for a second.'

'We shall see. In any case, do it soon, and let me know at once.'

I went home, phoned Pierre, and asked him to come and see me the next day, I needed to talk to him urgently about Sartre. He was worried, and wanted to know more. I held out, and reassured him, lying as best I could.

'No, no, Sartre is fine, I'll explain tomorrow.'

The next day Pierre arrived, looking worried. I asked him to sit down. As one often does, I had worked out how I meant to go about persuading him. But nothing went the way I had imagined. I was paralysed. The word, the word that was suddenly going to make Sartre become dependent – I couldn't utter it. Pierre became impatient, and kept tapping a cigarette nervously.

'Pierre, Sartre is practically blind. He can't read now, and he says he won't write any more . . .'

Pierre took off his glasses. He had tears in his eyes. I was very moved.

'You must give him three mornings a week from eleven to one, to read to him and help him to work. He'll pay you, of course.'

Pierre lowered his head, remained silent for a long time, and then said curtly: 'I've got things to do, I'll think about it, you've taken me by surprise.'

I was flabbergasted, beside myself.

'How can you dare tell me you've got things to do? You've squeezed him like a lemon for three years, you can certainly give him a few hours a week!'

'I've got things to do.'

'Pierre, you're forcing me to do something I've never yet done, and believe me, I'm finding it very difficult. I'm going to betray Sartre. He was the one who asked me to persuade you!'

After a few moments of silence Pierre obstinately repeated that he would think about it.

'You must say yes. Sartre is waiting for your answer. And after all, no one's asking you for any favours, you know how generous he is, this'll get you out of your financial difficulties. If I were you I'd be honoured to be asked by Sartre . . .'

'I feel I'm being trapped. I must think about it.'

'Too bad if that's the way you feel. I'm going to call him and tell him that you agree. He's waiting, don't you understand?'

Pierre stood up, looking stubborn. He picked up his brief-case and repeated, 'Even so, I've got things to do.'

As soon as he had gone I phoned Sartre, who luckily wasn't alone. So I could tell him that Pierre had agreed, without having to describe our conversation in detail.

The next morning, Arlette phoned me.

She yelled, 'What business is it of yours? Why did you persuade Pierre Victor to work with Sartre? You don't know Sartre. I've known him for fourteen years, I know what's good for him!'

She slammed the receiver down.

I hadn't had a chance to get a word in edgeways. I was furious. I was humiliated for Sartre that he had had to appeal to Pierre Victor, and I wasn't going to put up with Arlette's unjustified moods into the bargain.

I was torn between the urge to phone Arlette and tell her, 'And I've known him for thirteen years,' and the desire to protect Sartre. I decided to wait until the next day.

I was indescribably angry, and arrived at Sartre's late so as to avoid Arlette. Sartre had been told what had happened, and he was irritated.

'I've heard. Forget it, child, all these people are interfering with things that are none of their business. You know very well she thinks that everyone who hasn't come through her is a dog.'

'Even so, you're not talking about me, I hope. You know very well that I made a real effort. If it hadn't been for you . . .'

'Let's forget it, child. But tell me how it really was with Pierre.'

I hesitated. Ought I to tell him? How would he be able to take it? Sartre noticed my hesitation.

'Tell me the truth, child.'

'He took a bit of persuading. To tell you the truth, in order to persuade him, I betrayed you. I told him that the suggestion came from you. It was painful, you know. I wasn't particularly gentle with him, I didn't mince my words. I reminded him that they had all squeezed you like a lemon . . .'

Sartre laughed unreservedly.

'I had an idea it wouldn't be easy. I don't feel betrayed, that's the main thing! He's a bit reluctant, but he'll soon get to like it!'

'Shit. I'm sure there are millions of people who would pay to be with you!'

Sartre cut me short.

'Yes, but the thing is I don't want to work with just anyone!'

Sartre put his hand on my forearm, as he always did when he wanted to calm me or persuade me.

'It'll be all right, you'll see. Even with Arlette!'

'I don't give a damn about Arlette! I never want to see her again! If I meet her, I shall cross the road! Do you think I'm going to forget how she spoke to me? I hope she'll find out one day that it was your idea, and yours alone!'

'I shall be sure to tell her.'

'Be sure to, what does that mean?'

'Be sure to, that means that I shall be sure to tell her.'

'Why don't you say, "I shall tell her, you can be sure"?'

'Because it means the same thing.'

'That's what you say . . .'

I knew I wouldn't get him to change his mind, so I suggested we should put the books away.

'Don't forget that the Pléiades go in alphabetical order. You're a good girl, did you know?'

These words still torment me: why didn't I understand that in formulating them he had discovered that the complicity we so valued had just come to an end?

I looked at him. I was shattered, but I managed to get

out, 'Put some music on, will you please? I need to move, so as to calm down a bit.'

I was working out some plans while I dusted the books: we would find a way; I'd been told of a specialist in Holland who performed miracles without anaesthetic.

'Hm, you've got a new Pléiade volume?'

Sartre didn't answer; he'd dozed off. The phone rang and woke him abruptly.

'Hallo.' (His voice was just a whisper.) 'I'm fine, my dear Castor. Yes, I'm with Liliane, of course I'm expecting you at half past eight.' (His voice was back to normal.) 'Yes, all the best to you too.'

'Castor's worried, there was no reason for that phone call. Have I been asleep for long, child? What's the time? I can't see a thing on this watch.'

'I'll buy you another one. I can hardly see the time on your watch myself, there's no contrast between the colour of the face and the hands.'

The customary three little rings interrupted our laboured conversation.

I went and opened the door. Castor's worried eyes questioned me, and then she said to Sartre, 'Have you had a good day? Ah, I see you've tidied up the table!'

I took my jacket and bag, and left them without further ado.

I said no more to Sartre about how angry I felt with Arlette. But I always managed to avoid her when I arrived on Tuesdays.

A few months later, he said, 'Arlette isn't angry with you any more. She thinks that Pierre is doing well. She wants to get in touch with you and would like to know whether you'll respond. Come on, child, since she's the one who's taking the initiative. It's her way of apologizing, she realizes that she was wrong.'

'I know I'm going to say yes, but it's only for you.'

I still felt bitter, but Sartre wasn't his old self, he was dependent; my affection prevailed. I had a horror of injustice, but I wasn't going to complicate his life because of Arlette, even though she had ill-treated me for no reason.

And I finally grasped what Sartre had been trying to get me to understand for so many years.

'You and your LO-O-VE!

'To love, you have to know how to forget yourself, how not to put yourself first.'

His tone was abrupt, and then became mocking.

'What do you say to that, child?'

20

Sartre had envisaged the possibility of Arlette and me getting to know each other well before he introduced me officially into his life. 'Once the thing is done and Arlette has accepted it, I'm sure you'll be friends. You have affinities. It's true that she's suspicious, but if you hold your tongue it'll be a good thing for you both. You live near each other, you could go to the movies together and do lots of other things, you're alike in some ways. And after all, it was I who made you both!'

I was perfectly willing, and I imagine that he was working towards it with Arlette.

Her relations with Sartre are not my business. But our lives were closely linked to his. Sartre told Arlette about mine, with all the necessary lies, and he told me about hers, with no omissions but with the necessary advice: we mustn't give ourselves away.

What I was most afraid of in my conversations with Arlette was words. Sartre and Castor had their own private words and, without realizing it, over the years I had adopted them. When I was on my way home after being with Arlette I thought back to our conversation. I was panic-stricken, sure I'd let slip words like *le journaleux*, for the newspaper-seller; *la piqueuse*, for the nurse who gives injections; *une auto*; 'some *sous*'; and so on. And perhaps I had too often said, 'that's funny' or 'charming' and, who knows, all in the same evening!

I told Sartre about this the next day and it amused him. I protested.

'You're playing with fire, and it amuses you. But I assure you that I don't find it at all funny!'

'Maybe not, but don't forget that you are the dynamite!'

The first time Arlette came to see me, I took down all the photos of Sartre and Castor, but my heart missed a beat when I saw her looking at my books. I'd forgotten the dedications! I shall never know how I managed to put off an urgent call of nature: the WC was in the corridor, and I wasn't going to leave her alone. In her place I wouldn't have been able to resist it; I should have opened a book. Was Arlette so discreet, or would she rather not know? All Sartre's books were lined up next to all of Castor's, within arm's reach. I was relieved to hear her say a few moments later that she couldn't stay any longer.

Sartre had been surprised, but pleased. He had approved of Arlette coming to see me.

'She likes you, she hardly ever goes to see people!'

'That could be, but I'm not going to take it any further or I shall have a heart attack.'

'Not that, whatever you do. She wouldn't understand!'

And he burst out laughing.

Today, thinking back, I'm sure I gave myself away more than once. Nevertheless, even though our relationship was based on so many secrets, one thing is certain: for several years there was a very real bond between Arlette and me. Temperamentally, we were not made to get on with each other, and I think it was our attachment to Sartre that bound us together all that time.

The lies due to my ten years of clandestinity had been

imposed upon me against my will, by Sartre and for his own good, he claimed, but I was sincere with Arlette, except when she told me what she thought about Castor. When she did that, I prevaricated. I hated this, but Sartre encouraged it. 'Forget it, child, you'll never get her to change her mind. You'll turn her against you, and this isn't the moment. Don't forget that you're going on holiday together.'

This holiday, which Sartre had cunningly suggested, was a terrible ordeal for me.

We were in Arlette's house near Nîmes. Sartre phoned regularly, most often when we were on the terrace. The phone was in the adjoining room. Arlette answered it when it rang, which was only natural; it was her house. I could hear what she said and could easily imagine his part of the conversation. I began by stiffening. With each burst of laughter I could feel myself shrinking, until the moment when the conversation inexorably ended with, 'I'll be sure to. Goodbye, see you soon.'

Arlette would come back on to the terrace. 'Sartre sends you his regards.'

I would have liked to disappear.

One morning the postman brought a letter. I was on the terrace, Arlette joined me, with the letter in her hand, and sat down. I recognized Sartre's handwriting at once. I watched Arlette read the letter, protected by my sunglasses. For several days I had been trying to harden myself against the phone calls which I felt very clearly were irresistibly pushing me back into my former certainties: 'No one really loves me, they always let me down.'

It isn't easy to let go of the idea of yourself that you formed in your early childhood. I felt irritable and vindictive. Everything seemed ugly, 'inedible'. The sky was too blue, the nights too long. I felt sick.

It hadn't for a moment occurred to me to protect myself against this blow – the letter – and I felt the bottom had dropped out of everything. I felt cast off, betrayed. I knew I was in a trap, but I called myself a coward.

Arlette finished reading the letter, suddenly burst out laughing, stopped, looked at me and said, 'Sartre writes: "Write to me, you must, it will only cost you a stamp." He sends you his regards.'

I was beside myself, but I couldn't say a word. This time he'd see whether I was incapable of getting angry!

I made a vague excuse of having to go to the nearby village, and went and telephoned Sartre.

At the hotel, calls went through the operator.

'Madame Siegel is calling you.'

The man was efficient. So Sartre knew who was phoning him. When I heard his voice, I was incapable of uttering a sound.

'Hallo, child. I'm glad you called, I made a stupid mistake, I was just telling Castor, poor child, hallo?'

I was sobbing.

> 'They have turned their violence against themselves and are destroying themselves; reduced to impotence by their fathers . . .'*

'Hallo, child, say something!'

'When I think that it was you who wrote that!'

'But what are you talking about, what are you saying?'

'It's unbearable, that's what I have to say to you, what else can I do but destroy myself?'

'Nothing. Just do nothing. Leave everything the way it is. You only have two more days to hold out. Pull yourself together, I'll write to you this instant, you'll find

---

* Sartre's preface to Paul Nizan's *Aden-Arabie*.

133

the letter when you get back, I'll post it express and I'll phone you, that's a promise.'

A letter from Sartre was waiting for me in Paris:

> You could have written to me, but you hit back at me instead. I hope you'll find this letter when you get back, and answer it. Don't forget, though, that the Italian post is very slow ... It seems that Truffaut has written you an enormous letter (according to Gérald) ... And have you received the summonses?*
>
> Write to me without ill feeling and I'll make a fresh start – that's a promise.
>
> You can phone me here, the morning is a good time. But don't forget that there's an hour's difference between Paris and Rome.
>
> I'm well, am wearing my cap, have put on *6 kilos* (to be lost in two months).
>
> Castor and Sylvie send you friendly greetings, and I send you my love.
>
> J.-P.S.

---

* As co-editor of *La Cause du peuple*, I had been charged with libelling Raymond Marcellin, the then Minister of the Interior.

21

Sartre's health was becoming worrying. In the face of this threat hanging over him, my resentment disappeared. He had put on a lot of weight and I knew the risks he was running. Sartre had a tendency to high blood-pressure and he was pre-diabetic. He had several times had warning signs but he had a will of iron; he decided he would eat only once a day, and he kept to his decision. He obstinately decreed that he would eat nothing but steak *au poivre* with green beans until he had obtained the desired result: to lose the six kilos he had put on in Rome. It was useless for me to warn him, 'You'll ruin your stomach with all that meat and pepper!' He wouldn't listen. He lost six kilos in five weeks, and was very proud.

Every week he would tell me very happily, 'I've lost one kilo, two hundred grammes, Michelle weighed me!'

He had freely decided to reduce his intake of food, and didn't see this restriction as a sacrifice because it had led to an immediate and concrete result. For tobacco, on the other hand, the doctors didn't mince their words, and predicted the worst.

'If you don't stop smoking, you run the risk of having to have your legs amputated ...'

Castor and I were present. Professor X, who had just examined Sartre in another room, had been rather satisfied with his general condition.

There was an interminable silence. Castor slumped in

her seat. All I could hear were my own heartbeats. What was Sartre going to say?

He stood up, politely enquired how much he owed, and said, 'Thank you very much, Professor.' Then he added, curtly, 'Well, you two, are you coming?'

We were still sitting.

I had parked the car quite close, in the hospital court-yard. We walked to it in silence.

As soon as he was installed in the back, he flung at us in violent tones, 'And I don't want any of your bloody advice. I'll make my own decision.'

'That means that you're going to continue to smoke!' said Castor.

'Yes, for the moment, I must think about it. And then I'll come to a decision, but I don't want to talk about it any more.'

Quite some time before, Sartre had several times cut down his consumption of cigarettes. He had given up pipes a long time before, as well as cigars, which he particularly enjoyed, but later he had begun to smoke heavily again.

He stopped smoking out of generosity. One morning he told me at breakfast, 'I'm going to stop smoking, child, that'll be one less burden for Castor and for all the people who care for me. You can smoke, I want everyone to keep his habits, but I'm not convinced, you know. And anyway, I don't give a damn about my legs, it's my head that matters to me!'

I can still see his hands fumbling in his pockets or over the top of the low table by his armchair, trying to find his packet of Boyards. These so familiar gestures each time brought him back to the sad reality. 'Ah, I was forgetting, I don't smoke any more!'

If I'd known that this respite was only going to last two years!

22

Arlette had grown close to Pierre. I observed this change with amusement. They became friends. Pierre came less frequently 'to work' with Sartre. He was learning Hebrew with Arlette. I found him changed. He had a distant look, and an expression that spoke volumes, as Sartre would have said.

He lived in a suburban house in Groslay with his wife, his son and some friends: he pompously referred to it as 'the community'. He spoke of God too often.

I remember the day when, exasperated, I said to Sartre, 'Within three years he'll be wearing side-locks!'

'That's not impossible, but you're going a bit fast!' he replied, laughing unreservedly.

Where Pierre was concerned, Sartre had moments of total lucidity, and others of renunciation.

'Pierre would quite like to absorb me. Some days he baits me, we have a row, sometimes that amuses me and I stand up to him, but at other times it bores me so I give in. And as Arlette thinks that Castor is going to be the death of me, by encouraging me to drink, because she drinks too, he's become her ally. The obstacle being Castor, of course; he's no fool, you know!'

'I don't understand a thing any more. When you come back from Groslay you seem happy. You even go so far as to praise the cooking there. If anyone had told me that one day you'd go in for macrobiotics!'

'I don't go there very often, and anyway food doesn't matter so much any more. They go to a lot of trouble, you know. And anyway, it amuses me to watch Pierre's evolution.'

'You lie to him. But I thought you were fond of him?'

'I am, and I'm fond of Arlette too. You're asking stupid questions! Castor's the only person I never lie to, but it would take too long to explain. Don't you ever lie? And yet you're fond of them both!'

'It doesn't give me any pleasure . . .'

'I could quite happily do without it now, it doesn't amuse me any more. And in any case, I have a feeling that it isn't all that necessary any longer. All my lot meet each other, greet each other, and nothing terrible happens, as you see. Actually, apart from Castor, the only thing that entertains me is the new women who come to see me. The main thing is that I should be left in peace!'

From then on, Sartre spent 'Arlette's holidays' at her house in Junas. There were no more secrets, I could ask after him whenever I liked. At the end of his stay Arlette drove him to Nîmes and he flew from there to Paris. I was to meet him at Orly. I was delighted.

He was going to spend the day with me, sleep in Gérard's room, and stay until seven in the evening of the following day. After that, Bost* was going to take him to Wanda's, and then drive them to the airport. They were going to Italy, where Sartre was to meet Castor ten days later.

Castor phoned me to make sure that he had arrived and was well. She had made a meticulous list of the

* A former pupil of Sartre's who became and remained a friend of Sartre and Simone de Beauvour.

remedies to give him, and added a thousand instructions.

> Give Sartre:
> the usual medication (yellow tablets, red tablets,
> 25 drops Ezkedit)
> + before meals, 1 spoonful of the enclosed granules
> + 1 Anagarel tablet
> + 10 drops
> during the day, 1 tablet
> 2 eye-drops in the morning
> 2 eye-drops in the afternoon.

What agony she must have gone through with her Sartre dispersed during the summer!

I got to Orly very early, as I was afraid of missing him. He was always one of the last. I caught sight of his familiar silhouette in the distance. He was walking slowly, holding his bag in one hand and a straw hat in the other. I would so much have liked to run to meet him! He was looking straight ahead but he didn't see me. I forced myself to keep my hands together so as not to start waving. People walked past him, turned round and stared, hesitated, and then recognized him. 'Did you see, that's Sartre!'

I rushed up to the policeman checking the exit and dashed past, calling out to him as I went, 'It's Sartre, I'm meeting him.'

Then, to Sartre, 'Hi, did you have a good journey?'

I had got into the habit, ever since Sartre couldn't see, of talking to him as soon as I got near him so that he would recognize me.

'Ah, child, there you are! Yes, I didn't notice the time going by.'

But the time it took to get from the plane to me must

have seemed long to him, I thought. I tried to take his
bag.

'What are you doing, child, I'm still capable of carrying
a bag! You'd do better to relieve me of this hat, I'm
ashamed of it!'

'You've been telling me for years, though, that we
waste too much time getting rid of the idea of shame!'

'Oh come on, that's not the same thing!'

When we got to my place he sat down in 'his' armchair
and asked me to give him a whisky. I did so without
hesitation because for several months I had kept a special
bottle for him in the fridge which I had had no scruples
in diluting so that it was half water.

He told me about Junas, and asked what had been
happening in his absence.

'Only a fortnight now, and I'll be in Rome with dear
Castor. But these two days are for you, child, so it's for
you to decide. What would you like us to do?'

He said this in such touching tones that I was shattered.
But why had he got himself into such a mess? Why? I
kept my thoughts to myself.

'We'll go out for lunch, if you'd like to, but for tonight
I've got a surprise at home. All right?'

He smiled cheerfully.

'After your whisky you ought to go and have a rest.
There's some music on the bedside table, and anyway
you ought to change. There are some clean clothes in
Gérald's room. Leave your shoes in the hall. If you go
to sleep, I'll wake you at one, OK?'

'That suits me perfectly.'

A few moments later I was in the kitchen with Sartre's
shoes in my hand, trying to clean them. 'I shall never
manage, it isn't dust, it's dried mud ... What small feet
he has!'

I had turned the tap on and, brush in hand, I was scrubbing them, being careful not to get the inside wet. A greyish water dripped down, taking with it little mounds sticking to the sides and sole of the shoe.

'You'd do better to relieve me of this hat, I'm ashamed of it.'

'You've been telling me for years, though, that we waste too much time getting rid of the idea of shame!'

'Oh come on, that's not the same thing!'

He must certainly have been thinking of how others saw him. He probably felt ridiculous because he couldn't judge for himself, since he could practically not see at all. Yes, that was what he'd been thinking when he said, 'Oh come on, that's not the same thing!' If he could have seen himself he would have been free to decide, 'I think I look ridiculous so I'll take it off', or else, 'People think I look ridiculous so I'll keep it on, because I don't give a damn what other people think.'

But I was no longer in the Boulevard Raspail. I was a child again in the rue Chifflart, a cul-de-sac we lived in on the boundary of the 20th *arrondissement* and Les Lilas. We were very close to a school that we had been told was 'on the wrong side'. But the authorities didn't bother about such details. They sent us to the rue Pierre-Foncin, and we had to go a considerable distance to get to school.

In the summer we went off merrily along the streets that got the most sun. In the winter we arrived with our legs purple (girls didn't wear trousers at that time and tights didn't exist), our noses and ears red with cold, our fingers numb: gloves were a luxury that our parents couldn't afford to give us.

A glacial wind blew down the wide Boulevard Mortier.

In the autumn it was often raining, we found short cuts and walked as quickly as we could along the muddy pavements, soaked by the rain.

We arrived in a pitiful state and were often late. The pupils were already in the classroom, working. The moment my sister Léa, who was in the same class, and I came through the door, we were covered in shame by twenty-five pairs of inquisitorial, accusing and contemptuous eyes which stared at us pitilessly in the greatest silence until we got to our places. What a cold, unfeeling woman she was, 'our' mistress, who immediately added, 'Not only are you late, but you've covered the floor in mud! You must do a hundred lines, or would you prefer ten strokes of the ruler? You ought to be ashamed!'

Loud laughter from the whole class completed our humiliation.

'Well, child, I've just been listening to the news, it's after one, we must go and have lunch, what are you dreaming about?'

I hadn't heard Sartre come in; I jumped.

'I was wondering why I attached such importance to well-polished shoes!'

'What an odd idea. Incidentally, where did I put mine?'

We went to the Balzar for lunch. I read the menu for Sartre.

'Don't bother, child, I know what I want. Choose what you would like.'

'You'll explode with all that!' I said to Sartre when I heard him order a saveloy rémoulade, a sauerkraut, and a 'serious'.*

'I shall only eat the cabbage.'

'Shit, there's a guy coming up to us.'

* An enormous glass of beer.

'Ah? Who is it?'

'I know his face quite well, but I can't put a name to it.'

The man was standing in front of us and he greeted Sartre, who immediately said, 'You know . . .'

Sartre had no time to introduce me. The man nodded. 'Your daughter.'

'No, this one is my bastard!'

The man recoiled.

'Are you well?'

'My goodness yes,' Sartre replied, obviously enjoying himself.

'You're crazy,' I said, when the man had gone. 'You didn't see his expression, he was flabbergasted.'

Sartre laughed a lot.

'Your biographers and the historians will have a great time, I wonder how they'll be able to find their way between the letters you write Wanda from La Colombe d'Or*, telling her how you're working for peace in Vietnam, and . . .'

'You will tell them the truth! Actually, who was he?'

'François Châtelet.'

Sartre laughed heartily, and added, 'That's all right, he isn't too much of a gossip!'

By seven o'clock we were back in the flat. We were listening to France-Musique and Sartre was dozing in his armchair. I watched him sleep, and felt very moved. His head was on one side, slightly bent forward. How peaceful he looked! Suddenly I panicked. 'He's stopped breathing!'

Sartre gave a little moan, turned his head round to the other side, got his breath back and went back to sleep.

---

* A hotel in Saint-Paul-de-Vence.

'He's dreaming, of course. How stupid I am! Why should one always think the worst?'

The telephone interrupted my gloomy thoughts, and woke Sartre.

'Hallo? Yes, Castor, how are you, yes, he's here, of course I've given him his medicines, he's fine.' (Castor was asking so many questions that I couldn't follow her.) 'I'll put him on.'

I gave Sartre the receiver and disappeared into the room that was farthest away. I was shattered once again. Castor was worried too, I knew it! 'One day he'll die. I only hope it's not when he's with me!'

'Well then, child, that surprise – what is it exactly?'

'You gave me such a fright!'

'That's the price you have to pay for luxury, my poor child, your carpet deadens all sound!'

At eight o'clock Sartre listened to the television news, I laid the table and then went and did things in the kitchen. I hadn't been able to avoid the traditional whisky which he drank with pleasure, even though it was much diluted.

I turned on all the lamps, and put a particularly bright one very close to the table.

'Dinner is served, if Monsieur will be good enough to come to the table!'

'This is like the movies.'

'No, it's more like a fairy-tale.'

'What is this, actually?'

'Come on, taste it. After all this time, I know what you like!'

Sartre tasted it. He seemed suspicious.

'Caviar!' (He took some more immediately.) 'And good caviar!'

'Yes, it's beluga.'

'But where did you buy it?'

'At Dominique's.'

'Dominique's is closed in July.'

'I took my precautions, I bought it before they closed!'

'Ah, you're a good girl. How much for each of us?'

'A hundred grammes, as usual. Would you like a piece of toast?'

'Certainly not. You still don't understand, child, that you spoil it if you put it on bread. Where's the vodka?'

'One glass and no more, all right?'

'Don't start pestering me again. Unless you want to spoil things, bring the bottle.'

It had been too good to last, of course, and I had realized that there would be friction because of the vodka. I ought to have lied to him, to have told him I'd forgotten it. I had promised Castor that he wouldn't drink more than one glass. But he wouldn't listen.

I filled his glass.

'Aren't you drinking?'

'No. You drink enough for two.'

'Come on, child, don't sulk, you'll spoil everything.'

I looked desperately at his glass. It was already empty.

'I'll give you some *sous*, remind me to.'

'No, you're my guest.'

'Don't be silly, you'll ruin yourself.'

'And you are already ruined.'

'Ah, that's better, you're becoming caustic again.'

Sartre raised the glass to his lips, and then put it down on the table again.

'Give me something to drink, these glasses are minute.'

'The last, I warn you!'

'You warn me of what! You get on my bloody nerves the lot of you, trying to run my life!'

He had raised his voice.

'Alcohol isn't your life, it's your death.'

'So what? Everyone has to die.'

'It depends on what way.'

'That's none of your business.'

'Yes, it is! Can you see yourself bedridden, or gaga?'

'Forget it, child, we've been over that a hundred times. If that was the case, they'd kill me.'

'Oh yes? And who's *they*?'

'You, for example, supposing that you care about me enough!'

I was trembling with rage, helpless. Sartre was speaking coldly. I could feel the lurking threats.

'If you carry on like that, you can get out!'

This was always the ultimate argument in such cases. But he was at my place. I was incapable of reversing our roles, and searched desperately for a way out. This was how I had begun to betray him, to grass on him shamefully, as he said. It was my sole recourse.

'Give me the bottle.'

'This is what I'll do with your bottle!'

The window was wide open, and the bottle went flying through it and exploded four floors below.

Sartre roared with laughter. When he could finally speak, he said in a delighted voice, 'My goodness, you're coming on in leaps and bounds! All the same, you could have killed someone!'

I hadn't been expecting this reaction. I took it to mean that Sartre was giving in. How naïve of me!

He was very partial to rum babas, and a few moments later when I was putting one in front of him he placed his hand on mine and said, 'Come on, child, let's make up. I'll have a whisky later while we're watching the film!'

At nine o'clock the next morning Sartre was in fine fettle. I had hardly slept at all.

'Good morning, child, did you sleep well?'

'Very well. And you?'

'Never better. Are you ready? Come on, we'll go and have breakfast at the Select.'

'People might see us, the terrace is open in the summer.'

'Well, they'll see us then.'

It was pleasantly warm, the sky was magnificent. Sartre seemed happy. I forced myself to dismiss the clouds that would inescapably come to darken my day: in a few hours Bost would come to take him to Wanda's.

'Only a fortnight now, and I'll be in Rome with dear Castor,' he had said to me the day before in a strange way. There was a lump in my throat. But why had he got himself into such a mess? Why?

23

It was while they were in Rome that I heard the terrible news that Pierre Goldman had been murdered.

> 'There's only one way of telling people that some-one's dead, child. You start by saying, "He's dead," and then go on to describe the facts un-emotionally.'

I knew how fond Castor and Sartre were of Pierre Goldman. They were going to get a hell of a shock. Even so, I had to tell them. I phoned Rome.

Castor answered.

'Hallo, good evening, Liliane, how are you?'

She was so gay, I hesitated.

'Hallo, Liliane, what is it?'

> 'There's only one way of telling people that some-one's dead...'

'Castor, Pierre Goldman's dead.'

'Goldman? No – but how?'

She was sobbing so hard, it was terrifying. I couldn't understand a word she said, only that she was calling to Sartre, amid her tears, 'Goldman is dead! Goldman is dead!'

I could hear Sartre's irritated voice, asking, 'How? How did he die?'

Sartre came to the phone. I could hear Castor sobbing.

'Hallo, child. What happened?'

'He was murdered in the street.'

'Don't cry so loudly, Castor, I can't hear what Liliane is saying. He was what?'

'Murdered.'

'Murdered? How? Where? When?'

'With a revolver, in the street, barely an hour ago.'

'Do they know who?'

'No, he got away.'

'Well, shit, how bloody awful. Phone again when you know the date of the funeral. We'll be there.'

Castor and Sartre came to Pierre Goldman's funeral. Sartre was walking with difficulty, but he was determined to be there.

Sartre had always been totally opposed to any sort of self-indulgence. He had every right to this attitude: he himself was a permanent example that defied classification, and remained so until his death.

IV

24

The one subject I obstinately refused to talk about with Sartre was death. I went so far as to deny that it could exist. When Sartre insisted, I became pale.

'We'll have to talk about it one day, because logically, unless you get run over by a bus, I shall die before you. You ought to prepare yourself, it doesn't do any good to refuse to face reality.'

'Just see to it that you don't die. You know very well I've never seen a dead person.'

'Well, I'll be your first dead person.'

The moment I left him I became obsessed by the idea that Sartre could die. If he was ever five minutes late, as he was very punctual, I imagined that he was dead. When he went away I held my breath, I was terrified that I would hear of his death in the papers or on the radio or television, which I nevertheless kept up with assiduously. I couldn't breathe until I'd received the agreed telegram or phone call, which delivered me from the obsessive image of a crashing plane.

Wherever he went, he phoned me regularly during his stay, sometimes every day, and it was his voice more than anything else that enabled me to forget my fear of his death.

Later, when his health had begun to be really worrying, I was haunted by the idea that one morning, when going to fetch him for breakfast, I would be the one to find him dead.

It was a terrible blow for him when the project for his television programmes came to nothing.

But Sartre had resources that were as unforeseeable as they were unhoped for. Once he had admitted and accepted his near-blindness and his consequent dependence, he opted for life, and regained his gaiety.

I remember asking him one morning, at breakfast, 'Then it doesn't bother you too much, having to be dependent on other people?'

He smiled.

'No. There's even something rather pleasant about it.'

Physically, he was easily tired, but he still had a lot of activities and saw a lot of people. His strict timetable, which I had found such a burden in the days when he was writing, had gradually become more flexible. I saw more of him.

In different circumstances this would have been an unbelievable joy. But I was distressed by the successive visits to doctors, the hospital consultations and examinations which had become more frequent. Insidiously, fear took root in me.

In March 1977, Sartre, Castor and I were in Professor Housset's consulting-room and the doctor was looking through an enormous file: Sartre's medical notes.

For some time Sartre had been complaining of a pain in one foot; a severe pain, he said. He was so reticent about any sort of pain that I had deduced that it must be intolerable, and had panicked. Sartre had made me swear not to tell anyone, and he himself only mentioned it to Castor a few weeks later. A woman doctor friend of mine whom I had consulted had been pessimistic, and I had looked imploringly at Professor Housset so as to let him know that I knew, and that it might not be necessary to worry Sartre and Castor unduly, because that wouldn't change anything.

I was relieved to hear him congratulate Sartre on having stopped smoking. But he also said that Sartre should immediately stop walking whenever he felt a cramp in the leg, because he would run the risk of a heart attack or a stroke. The professor was quite categorical. He gave Castor an envelope, and took leave of us cordially.

From that day on my fear became obsessional, and never left me.

Castor and I took Sartre back to his flat and then went to her place, where we steamed the envelope open, but in vain. Doctors use hermetic terms deliberately. Castor then asked me to get in touch with my doctor friend.

The prognosis was very bad. Castor had made me promise to tell her the truth. I watered it down a little, but I reduced her to despair. Should I have lied to her? I still don't know the answer, and this question still torments me. Sartre was very much in demand, and in my opinion he took on far too much. But he needed to work, and for some time he had been complaining that Pierre didn't come often enough. He was happy to give interviews that he was keen on, but took no pleasure in others that were extorted from him. Lucid and generous, he scrupulously carried out certain obligations even though he found them boring chores. He had a very full life, and on the whole he seemed quite content.

Sartre was surrounded by many women, and he enjoyed himself in their company.

I had jealously kept him to myself for many years. He liked tête-à-têtes, and I didn't like sharing. On this particular point we were always in agreement.

When I heard that he was in real danger – 'If he's very careful he might live another year or two,' my doctor friend had told me – I made a radical change in my behaviour and decided to introduce some of my women friends to him.

He was all for it, but he asked me to describe them: he would choose. He had a lot of fun, and became twenty years younger! At this time he wasn't in the least interested in finding out why these women wanted to charm him, he couldn't care less. The only thing that mattered was that he should find them beautiful, even if only through my eyes.

The first one he chose was married to a man to whom she was terribly subjugated, whose meals she served meticulously, and whom she was never away from (she didn't work). She was lively and funny, but what particularly attracted Sartre, I think, was the idea that he would 'debauch' her – once he had been assured that she had a superb backside, of course.

She came twice; she was amazed to hear such straight talking! She took fright. She ran like a rabbit that fears for its life when it scents a hunter!

The second one was a teacher, younger, a brunette, pretty, she had a splendid body. She too was married, but to a man who lived his own life. Lucid, intelligent, funny, she liked talking about herself and wasn't afraid of words. Sartre found her attractive, she liked being with him, and they saw each other for longer. She had marital problems which she analysed judiciously, but according to Sartre she was refusing to face up to the most important thing. She had taken it into her head to find a place in the country which she would be able to do up with her husband. Sartre thought that the reasons she put forward to justify this new life were an alibi. She was also a painter. He explained to her bluntly and at length why she was faking herself.

She was good at repartee, had political opinions – the same as Sartre's – and she put them into practice. They should have had endless subjects of conversation.

She suddenly disappeared from his life.

'Be careful,' Sartre had told her. 'Because if you can't manage to paint in that house, which has no other positive feature to offer you, you'll kill yourself in it.'

It was clear that my endeavours had come to nothing. I decided to leave things at that and let Sartre pick his women for himself, he had plenty of choice. He had said one morning, 'Do you realize, child, that not counting Castor and Sylvie, there are nine women in my life at the moment!'

The only acquaintance he made through me, even though I didn't really want it to happen, was also the one that had the most serious consequences for me.

25

A woman had done me a big favour and I wanted to give her a present to thank her.

I didn't know her well enough and couldn't make up my mind. Naïvely, I decided to consult her.

'I'd like to give you a nice present, something that will last. What is there that you would really like?'

I can't even reproach her for having shown the momentary hypocritical hesitation usual in such cases. She replied immediately.

'A lunch with Sartre!'

'Why not a trip to Rome!' I thought. I was flabbergasted.

Sartre knew all about the favour she had done me and the present I was wanting to give her, and he was all for it. I indignantly reported our short conversation.

'She certainly has a nerve,' said Sartre, amused but vaguely flattered. 'What's she like? Is she beautiful?'

'More than beautiful.'

'Describe her to me.'

With a bad grace, I described her. She was a beauty.

'In that case we'll have lunch with her, in your time, next Thursday.'

We met at La Palette, a Montparnasse restaurant that no longer exists. Sartre invited her to sit next to him. I sat down opposite them and couldn't help thinking, 'He wasn't in the least interested in finding out why these women wanted to charm him, he couldn't care less. The only thing that mattered was that he should find them beautiful, even if only through my eyes.'

'It's overwhelming to be with such an intelligent person.'

These were her first words. I thought, 'She's mad. He's quite simply going to tell her to get lost.'

'Do you like Chablis?' Sartre asked her.

'Yes, very much.'

As she answered, she put her head on Sartre's shoulder. I couldn't believe my eyes.

'You can't possibly realize how much I admire you. I shall never forget this lunch.'

She simpered expertly.

'What would you like to eat?'

'Anything. I don't mind – so long as I am with you!'

With everything she said, she pawed Sartre, looking as if she was going to swoon. She was shameless. I was so embarrassed that every so often I tried to intervene. She overcame every obstacle.

'Why don't we order?' I ventured awkwardly.

'I'll read you the menu, shall I?'

'Why not?'

She'd called him *tu*! My goodness, in five minutes she'll be putting her hand in his pants!

The food and wine came. Sartre seemed to be enjoying himself. I wondered how this meal was going to end. I was nauseated. I didn't for a moment think of leaving the table, I hardly dared imagine what might happen, she was so shameless. Even so, a few moments later I had to disappear.

When I came back, she had become thoroughly vulgar, not to say pornographic. Garrulous, very much at her ease, she was telling Sartre about her sex life, not hesitating to include the smutty details or to cite names.

'It's four o'clock,' I said, getting the words out with difficulty.

Sartre had an appointment at his flat. He paid, she left us outside the restaurant, and I drove him home.

One morning a few days later, I gave Sartre his mail as usual and he asked me to read it to him because he couldn't see well enough.

Paris, November 26, 1979*

Dear Sartre,

That lunch was and is still a very important event in my life. I used to think that most of the time it was better not to talk too much because in any case one misrepresents oneself, and one's interlocutors misrepresent one's words, but I wasn't afraid with you. I shall be happy to continue this exchange on 13 December. I want to listen to you and I have heaps of things to tell you.

With much love

She had taken advantage of my absence that famous Thursday in the restaurant to get his address, and also to make another date.

She saw Sartre several more times, suggested he wrote a book on her sex life, and took him the whisky he asked her for.

Castor asked her coldly to stop doing so, and she complained to Sartre.

I had told Castor about her. I was not in any doubt as to what this would cost me – they told each other everything – but I preferred not to see Sartre and to know he was alive. I was afraid that if I said nothing it would hasten his end.

---

* Sartre asked me to take the letter away so no one could read it.

26

When Sartre found out that I was the one who had sneaked on him, he flew into a terrible rage. We had terrible scenes. He made all sorts of threats.

On 24 February 1980, he put them into practice.

'You make me sick, you're a filthy sneak. I never want to see you again.'

Castor was aghast at the severity of my punishment. Arlette tried to console me by telling me that he wasn't proud of himself, that actually I wasn't any guiltier than she was and he knew it, that he would calm down, and that she thought it was unfair. I was shattered.

I got news of Sartre from Castor or Arlette. March 11 was the anniversary of the day in 1961 when Sartre had declared that I was 'one of the family', and I asked Arlette to give him two Bach cassettes for me.

'He's calming down. I'm sure he isn't angry any more. He thanks you for your present.'

Encouraged by what Arlette had told me, on 20 March at half past nine, the time we usually had breakfast, I decided to phone Sartre.

I was terrified, torn between the misery he could cause me if he refused to speak to me and the possibility of a reconciliation, which I longed for.

The telephone rang. No one answered. I let it ring for a long time.

I knew Sartre was with Castor. It was too early for them to be at the café, I knew their habits. 'I must have dialled a wrong number, nerves probably ...'

I interpreted this in various ways. 'I shouldn't have phoned.' 'He knows it's me and doesn't want to answer.' 'Something's happened to him.'

I tried again, concentrating hard, but without success. I was overwhelmed with fear, incapable of making the slightest movement. I tried to think.

I had spoken to Castor the day before, they had been seeing Bost at Sartre's flat that evening. If anything had happened, if Castor had needed help, she would have called me, or Sylvie. But it was a Thursday, Sylvie left very early ...

No, it couldn't have happened the day before, Bost was with them. In any case, Castor would have let me know. I dialled the number again, but in vain. I phoned the operator. 'Monsieur Sartre's phone has been cut off, Madame, because his bill hasn't been paid.'

The secretary Sartre had engaged to relieve him of these contingencies didn't even take the trouble to pay the bills in time! 'Oof! I must tell Castor, we can't leave Sartre without a telephone.'

I got my breath back with some pleasure.

'That's typical of you, my poor child, you always imagine the worst!'

Sartre had said this to me so often!

I finally found Castor at home.

'Liliane, Sartre has been taken to hospital in an ambulance, he couldn't breathe.'

Her voice was choked with emotion.

'Oh, Liliane!'

I could hear nothing but her sobs.

'I'm on my way.'

I don't know how I managed to cover the two hundred metres between her place and mine. I rang her bell and she opened the door at once.

She threw herself into my arms, I let her cry. I held her tight. From time to time she said, 'Liliane, Liliane.'

She regained her self-control for a moment, sat down, became calmer, and told me what had happened.

'Would you like me to take you there?'

'He's having treatment.' (In the meantime, Castor had heard that he was at the Hôpital Broussais.) 'They wouldn't let me in, I'm waiting for the Pouillons, thank you.'

'Would you like me to tell Arlette?'

'Yes, please do, I don't feel like it.'

'Can I really leave you? Are you sure?'

She kissed my hand.

I found myself in the street, and finally managed to cry.

I have to admit that at that moment I was thinking, 'But how can Castor stay at home waiting? I would already have been at the hospital!'

Since then I have been in a similar situation and have come to realize that the time of hope, however short, that separates us from unbearable despair, is a vital respite.

I told Arlette the terrible news and offered to go and fetch her and drive her to the hospital. We lived very close to each other, and a few minutes later she was sitting in my *auto*. We didn't speak. After a long silence I managed with difficulty to tell her that I didn't know any more. Within a short time we were inside the hospital. I knew the way, alas; I had taken Sartre to see Professor Housset several times. But we had to find the intensive care unit – what is called *'le service de réanimation'*.

'That meant that they were resuscitating him . . .

'So he had lost consciousness . . .

'Would they manage to resuscitate him?

'What sort of state would I find him in?'

I was incapable of reasoning. I felt giddy, anguished. I looked at Arlette; she had turned yellow, she had a vacant look.

Everything was muddled in my head. I tried to put together what little I knew, and envisaged the worst.

'And what if he was dead, no, he couldn't be, he didn't want to be, he had no right . . .'

I had made up my mind: I wouldn't go in. He knew it, we'd agreed on it, I wasn't ready. We were on an upper floor, outside a closed door in a long, deserted corridor. I don't remember how long we waited. A group of men in white coats came up to us. All I remember is a few words uttered in a tone that chilled me.

'He's breathing more easily, but he's very tired. Only one person at a time. Who are you?'

'His daughter.'

Sartre had often told me, 'It's better to be a bastard daughter than an adopted daughter.' With the passing of time, to make peace, I had given up. But that day, stuck behind the door, terrified at the idea of not knowing, I painfully experienced the power of the sacrosanct family. And yet I had never felt so close to Arlette as at that moment. I was terrified at the idea of being left in the dark, I was relieved.

I managed to tell her that I would wait for her, and she disappeared at once.

From that moment on, my whole existence was devoted to waiting.

I waited for the news Arlette gave me, and the news I got from Castor and Sylvie.

Most of the time I went with Arlette to the hospital. I drove her home. The more I saw of her, the nearer to Sartre I felt. She gave me some reassuring news – he was eating, which for her was a good sign. For her part, Castor scrupulously reported to me what the doctors said. I had the feeling that she was forcing herself to believe them. I didn't dare ask her any real questions for fear of making things worse for her. Sylvie was very worried, she thought he was wasting away, was much thinner and weaker. I had no way of judging.

I would have given all the gold in the world to see Sartre for a moment. It seemed indecent to mention this to Castor. I knew that Pierre went to see Sartre with Arlette. They left just before Castor came in her turn, alone or with Sylvie, Bost, Pouillon or Lanzmann.

I imagined forcing my way in, or getting in unobserved in the middle of the night.

I had to see Sartre. Nobody could stop me. In actual fact, nobody was thinking of stopping me, but no one was in a position to realize how much harder it was for me. I hadn't seen Sartre since 24 February. He hadn't been on speaking terms with me when he went into hospital, and what if he was going to die!

I didn't know what to do, but my doctor worked at the Broussais hospital and I telephoned him.

'Tell me the truth, *please*. How is Sartre really? I can't see him. Is he in any real danger? Do you think I could go away for a few days, it'll be less painful if I'm not in Paris.'

'You can go, but don't go too far away.'

I thanked him as if he'd just given me the assurance that after all, Sartre wasn't in such a bad way.

I went on a sudden impulse, and regretted it immediately. At a distance, it was worse. I stayed obstinately in my room, sitting by the telephone. You had to go through a switchboard to get a number. It was agony.

Arlette phoned me several times. She thought he was better.

'He's allowed to sit in an armchair, and he's eating.'

It was a relief to hear Arlette, I felt linked to Sartre through her, but what she told me seemed to stem more from obstinacy than from clarity.

Finally I managed to get hold of Sylvie.

'What! Didn't you know, Liliane? Sartre is in a very poor way!'

I went back at once and found Arlette exhausted but confident.

On the evening of 14 April I went to the hospital with Arlette and went into the room with her. Sartre seemed to be asleep.

He was so pale, thin, transformed, that I was certain he was going to die.

Arlette went up very close to him.

'It's Arlette, I'm with Liliane.'

Sartre opened his eyes, he hadn't got his glasses on. I was on the other side of the bed. I went nearer, kissed him on his upturned cheek – he had turned his head towards me.

'Ah, it's you, Liliane, and how are you?'

He was speaking with difficulty. Arlette, seeing that I hadn't understood, translated for me. I was leaning over him.

'You smell good.'

I was holding back my tears and didn't know what to say.

'Yes. Arlette brought me some citronella toilet water.'

He pronounced these words clearly, and closed his eyes. I looked at Arlette; her eyes were full of despair.

Sartre didn't move any more, he seemed to be asleep. We stayed there for a long time in silence, sitting on either side of the bed. No one came and asked us to go, we left of our own accord, for no reason.

At this stage of the story I am incapable of remembering what happened until the moment when I went to fetch Arlette in the late afternoon of 15 April.

I didn't go in to see Sartre that day, I waited for Arlette on the landing. My friend Dominique had phoned me, 'Lili, he's going to die, and believe me, it's better that way.'

When Arlette came out, I said:

'You had better stay.'

'Do you think so? But why?'

The doctor I knew appeared at this moment, and answered my question in a tone that he tried to make neutral, 'If you want to, you can.'

I left her and went home, where my friend Dominique was waiting for me. She hadn't slept for forty-eight hours and I thought her presence was suspicious. She was busy in the kitchen.

'We'll have something to eat.'

The phone rang. It was Arlette.

'Liliane, it's over.'

'What do you mean, "it's over"? You mean he's dead?'

'Yes. Tell Castor. I can't.'

Dominique took me in her arms.

I shouted, 'No, it's not true, I'm sure they're mistaken!'

'Castor, Castor must be told.'

We drove off as fast as we could. No one at Castor's place. No one at Sylvie's.

'Come on, Mimique, we'll go to the hospital, I'm sure Castor's there.'

167

It was terrible outside the hospital. Television crews, journalists, photographers. The gate was closed. Dominique got out of the *auto* and asked the doorkeeper to open it, telling him that I was a member of the family. He didn't want to know. She ordered him to phone the department where Sartre was and gave him my name. He obeyed, and let us in. I caught sight of Sylvie and called her name. She looked at me and yelled, sobbing, 'He's dead, Liliane!'

'I've never seen a dead person.'
'Well, I'll be your first dead person.'
'Just see to it that you don't die.'

I remembered these remarks as I walked, supported by Dominique. I stood still for a moment, looked at Dominique, removed her arms.
'Are you sure?'
She moved away. I went into the room. Sartre seemed to be asleep. I went up to him. He was so pale. I hesitated, I felt my legs giving way.

'You know, child, a dead person looks like someone who's asleep. It isn't so terrible, you know. What's terrible is the fact that he's dead.'

I placed the tips of my fingers on his cheek, it was warm. I clung on to the bars on the bed.
'You weren't made for this.'
I hadn't noticed Arlette. She was sitting on the other side of the bed, repeating these words like a litany, and sobbing.
Then I saw Castor. I threw myself into her arms and managed to cry. Shortly afterwards Sylvie came back, followed later by Bost, Pouillon, Le Whyshie, and Lanzmann, who kept stroking Sartre's feet and saying, '*Mon petit, mon petit.*'

Bost walked up and down, repeating, 'It isn't true, it just isn't true.'

I only have a very vague memory of all this.

We were asked to leave; it was five in the morning. I caught sight of Dominique in the corridor. She had stayed there waiting for me. We gave Arlette a lift, that went without saying. When we got to my place, as we were getting out of the *auto* a man rushed up to Arlette. She hit him. It was dark.

'Arlette, it's me, Pierre.'

She didn't listen, and went on struggling. She had taken him for a journalist. Pierre told us that he had been to the hospital and had been told that we had just left. He was with a woman friend, he didn't drive.

We went up to my flat. Pierre asked Dominique to make some tea, sat down on the carpet beside Arlette and took her in his arms. No one spoke. After a time, Arlette said she wanted to go home. Pierre stood up and they left together.

Dominique was furious.

'What's he thinking about, your Pierre! I thought he was supposed to be your friend, what he's doing is disgusting. He's already muscling in, he isn't wasting any time!'

I was thinking only one thing: without Arlette, I should never have seen Sartre alive again!

I have practically obliterated everything that happened between that time and the burial.

I was anaesthetized, keyed-up for what I thought of as the end. I had forgotten nothing of the two deaths that had shattered me – that of my mother and that of my nephew. After the shock, you veer between the feeling of 'Nevermore' and the inability to believe it.

Grief and loss cannot be measured; to each his own share. I imposed a certain restraint on myself where

Castor was concerned. To enquire after her other than through Sylvie would have seemed indecent. I knew that Sylvie never left her for a second. I felt very much alone.

Pierre didn't show up. I vaguely remember having gone to see Arlette several times, and always finding Pierre there.

During my 'quarrel' with Sartre, relations between Pierre and Castor had been broken off because of the famous article in *Le Nouvel Observateur*.* Arlette had taken Pierre's side against Castor, and had lost no time in feeling herself invested with a certain importance, as Sartre would have said.

I particularly remember the day when, leaning back in her chair, she came out with a remark that left me speechless: 'Castor wants him for herself, now that he's dead.'

'Take some tranquillizers,' Dominique had advised me. 'It's hard when they put the lid on.'

I looked without seeing. No, that man in the box, he wasn't 'my' Sartre, I was having a nightmare, I would wake up and tell him about it.

'Why did you "choose" to make me die?' he would ask me.

'But I don't want you to die, nor do you, for that matter, you'd promised, you said, "Another ten years at least."'

The men arrived, it seemed to me that they were making a noise in this 'deathly silence'. I looked away. No, surely they weren't going to shut him up in that packing case! He so loved the light, the sun, colours . . . I felt my legs giving way.

* See above, p. 108

'You make too much of it, child . . .'

I found myself behind the hearse they had slid him into, I felt even shakier on my feet. Two big gates opened on to the street and a mass of humanity flooded into the forecourt. People were jostling one another, jostling me, I felt myself being caught up, lifted off the ground, and then I was sitting in a coach. My son was stroking my hair, his wife was holding my hands.

I heard later that there had been a lot of people; I hadn't seen anyone. The coach went past my block, past the café where we had so often had breakfast together. I was empty, I didn't feel a thing.

A few details come back to my mind: in the cemetery I thought I was at a demonstration and that Castor was going to be suffocated. I got into an *auto* with Castor, Sylvie, Lanzmann and Arlette; I had the impression that the driver thought he was competing in a Formula-One race – probably in comparison with the snail's pace we'd been going at before.

I found myself in the street, alone, and I fainted. A woman picked me up, another took me home. A friend was anxiously waiting for me there; I threw myself into his arms.

I didn't know that the worst was yet to come.

The cemetery was deserted. A few of us who had been very close to Sartre were standing in front of a mountain of flowers. Pierre wasn't there. He hadn't come the day the body had been put into the coffin, either. Castor was exhausted and had allowed Sylvie and her friends to persuade her not to come to the cremation. For me, the burial the previous Saturday had been the proof of Sartre's death. Oddly enough, when they took the coffin out of the grave to put it into the hearse, I was convinced that I was having another nightmare and that I would wake up and tell him about it. I could already hear him protesting tenderly:

'Oh come on, my poor child, why do you choose to encumber your life with my death, I'm well and truly here, for at least another ten years.'

I had never been to a cremation. The very word gave me the shivers. Many members of my family were exterminated by the Nazis at Auschwitz, as well as my sister Bella.

When the doors slid open and revealed the flames, and when the coffin made its way into them, I realized why my mother had died of despair. Sartre was dead, I had seen him dead, he couldn't feel anything. I could see my mother, sorrowfully stroking the dog (it was all we had left of my sister):

'If only I was sure that she died beforehand!'

We were asked to go up to the first floor, it would take a long time. It was interminable. You could hear the sound of the furnace. I would have liked to scream but I couldn't even cry, I was dried up. My head was spinning, I fought against it, I felt I was going to faint, I would have liked to faint, and forget for a few moments, a few seconds. I thought of Castor, they shouldn't have left her alone, it's always more difficult when you're not there.

'Come this way, please. The ashes are going to be put into the urn.'

I remained glued to my seat. A few people went down. I heard a scraping sound. They were shovelling up the last traces of the ashes. I could see Sartre in my flat, in an armchair in front of the hearth.

'Clear the ashes away, child, you can see the fire's going out.'

They came for us. We were petrified at the sight of the 'vase' they put in the hearse that had previously contained the coffin. The contrast was so striking that it seemed to me ridiculous that we should be told to form a cortège.

'A tiny little can, that's all that's left of you, my poor little Sartre.'

We drove across Paris, from Père Lachaise to the Montparnasse cemetery. Every so often we lost sight of the precious cargo. I looked up at the sky, where the wind was sweeping great clouds away, presenting me with big blue open spaces.

'I hate the sky when it's blue . . .'
'You'll have to learn to get used to it.'

Twenty years had gone by.

We had arrived at Sartre's tomb. Sylvie was between Arlette and me, firmly supporting us both.

The grave was very deep. I don't remember how Sartre's ashes were placed in it, and I don't remember either who asked for them to be moved so that they would be better protected.

Everyone threw a flower into this abyss, all of us found it difficult to tear ourselves away.

Pierre was waiting at Arlette's. He asked questions. Arlette was having trouble breathing, she could hardly speak. Her voice became full of gratitude when she said very persuasively to Pierre, 'You know, Sylvie really looked after us.'

Pierre detested Sylvie, and interrupted Arlette brusquely. It was quite clear that he didn't want to hear her sing Sylvie's praises.

'And Michelle?'

Pierre had no real connection with Michelle. I immediately understood the meaning of this spiteful interruption.

Arlette stiffened and said no more. I was exhausted and went home, avoiding the gaze of the people I met in the street. They had seen me too often with Sartre. I could do without their morbid curiosity and their compassion. I needed to be alone.

Sylvie phoned me.

'Liliane, Castor is in hospital. When Lanzmann and I got back to my flat she had fallen out of bed, she was delirious. She has pneumonia.'

I was aghast.

My relations with Castor had been built up very gradually, according to her wishes. Everyone his own friendships, as Sartre used to say at the very beginning.

My affection for Castor had arisen as a matter of course when I was reading *The Prime of Life*, although I didn't altogether realize it at the time. I had never known anything like the dimension of their love for each other; their tranquil certainty that only death could separate them, their absolute confidence in the future and the authenticity of their relationship – all this aroused a feeling in me that has never changed. They were indissociable, and I loved them as a single entity, but this entity, amputated from Sartre, was now lying in hospital.

Where would Castor find the desire, the energy necessary to get better? I had a confused feeling that in some way Sartre would go on living so long as Castor was alive.

I was very worried, but I remembered something Castor had said:

'It's terrible not to be there to comfort people for the grief you cause them by leaving them, it's terrible that he abandons you and remains silent.'

Castor was too fond of Sylvie, I thought, to inflict this second ordeal on her. I considered Sylvie her breath of life. Sylvie's determination that she should live, her vitality, and above all her love would see Castor through.

I got news of Castor from Sylvie; I was waiting for her to get better before I went to see her. When I went into her room I was relieved to see that she was practically cured of her pneumonia. But her look had changed, her eyes had become pink. I felt she was fragile; she worried me a lot.

The media had reported the fact that Castor was in hospital, so I was amazed to hear from Sylvie that Arlette had never enquired after her.

I stayed at home for weeks in a state of prostration. My daughter-in-law screened my phone calls; I was pursued by certain journalists who were hoping I would let something slip. My friends had sent telegrams and touching letters, and now they enquired after Castor. But there was no sign of either Arlette or Pierre.

I phoned Pierre and complained about his silence. We had been very close; didn't he understand my need to talk to him about Sartre? He seemed distant and vague, but in the end he gave in and came to see me.

I described my solitude to him.

'I can't talk to just anyone about the gap Sartre's death has left.'

'You can come to Groslay whenever you like.'

'But there's Arlette. No, I don't want to lie any more, there's no more reason to now.'

'If that's all it is, do you want me to tell her? No problem. Incidentally, are you going to keep in touch with Castor?'

I asked after Arlette.

'She's very busy, a lot of things to do, and then Sartre's flat will have to be vacated. Is there anything you'd particularly like from it?'

I replied automatically, without realizing the importance it would take on later. He stood up.

'I must go.'

'I'll come as far as the *tabac* with you.'

He walked on, and I was sobbing as I watched him. I was in torment, I ought to have gone with him. I imagined naïvely that he was going to visit Sartre's grave. I went up to my flat and the phone rang.

'It's Pierre, I'm at Sartre's place with Arlette. Unfortunately, your mother's bedside lamp and the radio have gone, but you can have the rug and the Giacometti lamp . . .'

'What d'you mean they've gone? What lamp?'

'You know, the floor lamp.'

'You're crazy. *I* bought that in the flea market. It's my mother's one I wanted, it's all I have left of her.'

Half an hour later, I was brought the floor lamp, the rug, and the low, smoked-glass table Castor had bought Sartre.

Dazed, I looked at these objects taken out of their setting, and realized just how far I had been duped. So when he left me, Pierre had been going to meet Arlette to 'vacate' Sartre's flat, and had taken good care not to tell me.

I was revolted by so much deceit and indecency. How had they dared get their hands on Sartre's furniture, books and intimate objects without waiting for Castor to be the first to decide? Castor was in hospital, and nothing could justify such haste.

Sylvie told me that Castor was shattered. She wanted Sartre's chair, the one that had come down to him from his great-grandfather, and she had been refused it.

'Don't worry, I'll get it.'

I phoned Arlette and told her I wanted to see her. She told me she was very busy but I insisted. She arranged to meet me at the Dôme four days later. Arlette always saw me at her place and had never before made the excuse of being too busy to see me. I knew how she spent her time, and I knew what she was like: her hesitation and wariness were significant, and indicated that our meeting would not go particularly smoothly.

'You know why I wanted to see you? I've come to ask you for the chair. Castor is particularly attached to it.'

'So am I particularly attached to it.'

'How can you compare yourself with Castor? Do you think Sartre would have wanted that?'

'You've come to lecture me . . .'

'I've come to ask you for the chair, you've no right . . .'

'I'm just as attached to that chair as she is.'

She stood up. I followed her, and we walked side by side in silence. At the corner of the rue Delambre she stopped, and said in cutting tones, 'You can tell her she can have it!'

Twelve days later, an unknown person rang Castor's doorbell and left the chair.

Who does not know what the hours, the days, the nights are like that follow the incurable absence of a beloved person? Streets, places, smells, music – all are to be avoided, yet are unavoidable. But the armchair is there, *his* armchair. Everywhere you look you can feel his presence, hear his voice, and they bring back whole sequences of life which were so happy, but which death has transformed into despair.

All the 'first times' without Sartre plunged me deeper into despair. The first slice of bread and butter which I was just going to put into my mouth – I flung it on to the ground. My first holiday was a dismal failure. When I came back I had made up my mind: I would move, I would go somewhere else.

Castor dissuaded me. She was grief-stricken but she was still working. Self-effacement was called for.

27

I saw Castor regularly during the six years she survived Sartre. I would have done anything for her; I did everything she would allow me to.

I loved Castor, and I believe she liked me.

After Sartre's death I turned to her for counsel. She advised me on my reading, helped me organize my holidays, urged me to see certain films, comforted me, invited me to excellent restaurants with Sylvie. She was so like Sartre in the way she was with me that I gradually began to plunge back into fear: what if she were to die!

Sylvie had told me what Castor had been living through since Sartre's death, but when I took them both to the clinic on 15 April 1982, I knew for certain that without Sylvie, Castor wouldn't go on living.

Sylvie had broken her ankle in London, where it had been put in plaster. When she got back to Paris she had it X-rayed.

I took Castor home, she would have had to wait too long, and went back to Sylvie. The verdict was that she needed an operation. I didn't want to tell Castor this over the phone so I went back to her place.

When she heard the news, she collapsed. She sobbed, and moaned, 'No, not Sylvie, not my Sylvie, not today . . .'

I knelt down, and she threw herself into my arms.

'What if she doesn't wake up, not today . . .'

She wept for a long time, and asked me to take her to see Sylvie. I knew it was too soon, but I agreed. Sylvie's bed was empty. Castor kept looking at her watch. I tried to reassure her.

'I told you it was too soon.'

Sylvie was finally brought in. She wasn't completely conscious. Castor panicked. The nurse calmed her down.

'Don't worry, she's coming round very well. Come on, Mademoiselle, open your eyes.'

We were on either side of the bed. Sylvie opened her eyes and swiftly took our hands at the same moment. Castor was finding it difficult to keep back her emotion. Sylvie saw this, and began to speak:

'Castor, Liliane, I saw some blue . . . a lovely blue . . .'

She talked and talked, and finally made us laugh. After a long while she was completely awake, she saw that Castor had been crying.

'Castor, you must go home and give poor little Liliane something to eat, she hasn't eaten all day.'

She squeezed my hand very hard, to make me understand, as I did right away, that whatever happened I mustn't leave Castor alone. Reassured, Castor agreed to go home. Sylvie had prepared our menu; the freezer was full of food.

Castor chose a good bottle of red Bordeaux, and in the intimacy of her little kitchen, our meal, my first meal at Castor's, was almost joyful.

Sustained by Sylvie, Castor began working again, and life seemed to be going on in spite of everything.

1986:

'Hallo, Liliane,' (I recognized Sylvie's voice) 'believe it or not, Castor is in hospital, the doctor had her rushed there with acute appendicitis. I'll phone you again to-night.'

They gave Castor a lot of tests but didn't operate. I had a dreadful presentiment. Why hadn't they operated? The diagnosis was relatively simple . . . True, an anaes-thetic at her age is a risk, but an emergency is an emergency . . .

What was the next catastrophe going to be? Castor had an operation, but it was followed by complications and she was taken into intensive care. The nightmare began again.

Sylvie kept me in touch regularly: the news varied from day to day, from hour to hour. I veered between hope and despair.

When April arrived, my presentiment became intoler-able. Sylvie seemed to be strong, I didn't discourage her.

One evening towards midnight Sylvie felt she wanted to see Castor. We sneaked in like practised thieves. Castor was lying on a bed in the middle of an overheated room, asleep. I hadn't seen her since she had been admitted to hospital. I watched her breathe, and realized that she was going to die.

On 14 April at three in the afternoon, Sylvie phoned me.

'Liliane, I'm at the hospital. Castor has just died.'

I knew she wouldn't live to see another 15 April. I rushed to the hospital, and no one stopped me from going in.

I stared at Castor's face, convinced that she was going to open her beautiful blue eyes. I don't know how long we stayed there without exchanging a word, without shedding a tear. We were asked to leave; I think they were going to take Castor away. I told Sylvie I'd go with her wherever she liked.

'Would you mind if we went to Castor's?'

'Of course not.'

I looked round the room Castor had lived in. Everything was in its place, I couldn't believe she would never come back.

Sylvie wanted to see Castor again and I went with her. We went into the amphitheatre and she told them who she was. They wheeled Castor in; she was wearing a red dressing-gown.

With a naturalness that will for ever be a lesson to me, Sylvie asked me to raise Castor's head so that she could put her headscarf on. I took the icy face in my hands and raised her head. Patiently, tenderly, as she had so often done before, Sylvie tied the red scarf round Castor's face for the last time.

> 'You know, child, a dead person looks like someone who's asleep. It isn't so terrible, you know. What's terrible is the fact that he's dead.'

Dear Liliane,

I think of you very often these days, even when I'm shooting. A third stage of your life is beginning now. He taught you to live without your mother and, if you remember only the best things, I believe he will also have taught you to live without him. And then, never lose sight of the fact that he was spared any real decline. Your nephew's death is a scandal but Sartre's isn't, it's in the chronological order of things. Life is you, Gérald and little Emily, *that* is what must take priority. If this letter comes too soon, forget it as soon as you've read it, but remember that I am with you.

François